Window Treatments *For Every Room*   John Wiley & Sons, Inc.

For general information about our other products and services, please contact our Customer Care
Department within the United States at (800) 762-2974, outside the United States at (317)
572-3993 or fax (317) 572-4002.

Wiley also publishes its books in a variety of electronic formats. Some content that appears in
print may not be available in electronic books. For more information about Wiley products, visit
our web site at www.wiley.com.

ISBN 978-0-696-22552-9

Printed in the United States of America

10 9 8 7 6 5

Note to the Readers:
Due to differing conditions, tools, and individual skills, John Wiley & Sons, Inc., assumes no
responsibility for any damages, injuries suffered, or losses incurred as a result of following the
information published in this book. Before beginning any project, review the instructions carefully,
and if any doubts or questions remain, consult local experts or authorities. Because codes and
regulations vary greatly, you always should check with authorities to ensure that your project
complies with all applicable local codes and regulations. Always read and observe all of the safety
precautions provided by manufacturers of any tools, equipment, or supplies, and follow all
accepted safety procedures.

Preceding page: Elegant
chinoiserie toile takes on
charming cottage style when
bordered in gingham and
hung on a window amid
wide, painted wall planks.
To see other ways to dress
windows with toile, turn to
pages 41 and *49.*
This page: Open blinds
bathe a bathtub in sunlight.
The slats tilt closed for
complete privacy. To learn
more about blinds, turn to
pages 22 and *23.*

contents

introduction

British designer Mary Gilliatt once said, "Windows are like eyes—they are looked at as much as they are looked out of."

And like your eyes, windows offer an intimate glimpse into your personality, revealing your sense of style. With their notable status, windows deserve particular consideration in your decorating plans throughout the house. That's why this book is organized for convenience: Chapters focus on specific types of rooms—gathering rooms, kitchens and dining rooms, bedrooms and baths, and special spaces, such as home offices, window seats, and home theaters—so you can quickly find treatments that meet the functional and aesthetic needs of each space. Within each room category, a variety of looks—from contemporary to traditional and casual to formal—is depicted in beautiful interiors to capture your imagination and give you ideas for dressing your windows with style.

But this isn't just a book of pretty pictures. You'll learn why every treatment works well in each room and what features make it functional. That way, you'll know which types of treatments will best meet your needs.

When you're ready to begin measuring, choosing fabrics, and picking out hardware, turn to the "Decorating Pantry" on page 90. You'll be delighted by the enormous design opportunities as you become armed with the knowledge to whittle down choices when shopping for ready-made treatments at a home center or through a catalog. Knowing terminology commonly associated with window treatments also will come in handy if you opt for custom treatments designed by a workroom.

The book also includes an attractive assortment of easy-to-make window treatments and embellishments, beginning on page 110. Whether you love to sew or are handy with a hot-glue gun, you will find a project that will add a special touch to your home.

Enjoy this journey as you peer into the "eyes" of countless homes. You're sure to discover the window treatments that offer the exact purpose and personality you desire.

Unpretentious panels—fashioned from fabric with an oversize blue-and-white cabbage rose motif—pair with the ticking-striped sofa to play up the relaxed country character of this room *opposite*. One panel is pulled back to keep the look even more casual.

gatheringrooms

Window treatments play a primary role in communicating the look and feel you want for your living room, family room, or great-room. This chapter will inspire you with a wide range of options, whether your style is formal and traditional or casual and contemporary. You'll also find ways to control privacy, sunlight, and views without sacrificing great design.

floor-to-ceiling elegance Take the style of your living room, family room, or great-room to new heights with fabric window treatments that stretch from the top of the wall to the floor. This technique lures the eye upward to emphasize the drama of a high ceiling, such as in the living room *below*, or creates the illusion of a much grander space. Hanging panels at ceiling height also can lend symmetry to a room with varying window heights, sizes, or styles, as in the family room *opposite*. Play up the desired effect by accentuating the top of a window treatment with decorative hardware or fabric embellishments. The wooden rings at the top of the toile treatments *opposite*, for example, are a bonus worth looking up to.

comfort&style

2

① The intricate latticework of a smocked header adds an eloquent handmade touch to these Belgian linen draperies. The smoky blue hue and subtle details suit the understated elegance of the room. Delicately edged with sterling-silver beads, the fabric panels also feature hidden cords, called Italian stringing, that draw the panels to the side to welcome sunlight.

② Rounded specialty windows pose a particular challenge if you want to block intense sunlight. These floor-to-ceiling panels attractively resolve the issue for a matched pair of transom-topped French doors. Rather than a separate pole for each set of doors, one long decorative rod spans the openings—and beyond—so the panels can be pulled back to each side of the doors. Substantial wood rings slide along the rod, offering a casual contrast to the pink toile fabric.

● ON PAGE 6 White-painted shutters swing on hinges to open the window to a full view, sunlight, and breezes. To learn more about shutters, turn to *pages 46* and *47.*

If you're searching for a treatment that's stylish, functional, and easy on the budget, consider shades. Compared to full-panel treatments, shades use minimal fabric, yet they still provide privacy and block light. Raised shades welcome sunlight and views while still softening the hard lines of the window, such as the festoon shades *opposite*. Pull the shade down to fully conceal the window and bring added color to the space. Select more tailored (clean-lined) looks for small rooms or to prevent the treatment from competing with furnishings in any size room, such as the tie-up shade *below left*. Use gathered or embellished shades to create a focal point, such as the translucent roller shade *below right*.

fashionableshades

❶ Add shape to a boxy room with curvaceous festoon shades. These repeat fabric used on the window seat below. When drawn up, a festoon forms a festive valance with tails on the ends and a swag in the middle. Two cords strung vertically through rings on the back of the fabric allow the shade to be raised and lowered.
❷ Complement a casual decorating scheme with the understated styling of a tie-up shade. Composed of a flat panel with no drawstrings or plastic rings, a tie-up shade hangs from a rod or mounting board. Raise and lower the shade by hand as you roll it, fold it, or scrunch it; use the ties to hold the shade at the desired height. The gauzy fabric used for these shades suits the

contemporary setting. The subtle checked pattern echoes the crosshatch design on the walls.
❸ Do-it-yourself roller shade kits, which are available at crafts and fabrics stores, let you create a custom roller shade. Typically, kits contain a roller tube, hanging hardware, fusing material, and instructions. This shade was fashioned from a beautiful transparent wallcovering that was the same width as the window and fit perfectly on a roller tube. You could also iron your favorite fabric to the fusible backing that attaches to the roller tube. For a shade that allows light to filter through, skip the fusible backing and secure sheer fabrics or lace directly to the roller tube.

cornice crowns

Introduce architecture to an ordinary gathering room by topping a window with a cornice assembled from plywood, wood screws, and corner brackets. A cornice hangs at the top of the window (secured to the wall just beyond the trim) and protrudes 6 to 8 inches from the wall. Dress the cornice with moldings and paint, as shown *left*, or use fabric or wallcoverings. You can also add embellishments, including wood on-lays, cording, or fringe, as shown *opposite*. Let the structure stand alone, or pair it with fabric panels, blinds, or a shade for privacy and light control (and to attractively conceal the tops of blinds or shades).

❶ Hand-painted butterflies flit among the lines of a tricolor plaid design on this wooden cornice, which serves as a playful touch for a casual gathering space. Designs such as these let the structure function as artwork. If this look appeals to you but you don't care to paint freehand, use stencils or stamps to decorate the surface. Or simplify the design with painted polka dots, which easily can be made with an inexpensive foam dauber. This cornice also features mitered strips of molding for added dimension.

❷ Soften a wooden cornice with layers of batting and add texture or color with a fabric covering. A layer of muslin puts this ¼-inch-thick plywood cornice under wraps. The edges of the fabric are pulled around and stapled to the back of the wood. Hot glue secures rows of ball fringe (about 35 yards) across the front and sides of the cornice. Additional pom-pom fringe adorns the panels and tiebacks. The result is a fun focal point for this casual living room.

1 Three layers of fabric—a top, lining, and flannel interlining—make these valances swoop and cascade with ease. The softness of the treatments couples with the substantial rods and rings to balance the casual wicker furnishings with a note of luxury.

2 Fabric valances conform perfectly to these arch-top windows, offering interest without concealing the view or detracting from the remarkable woodwork around the windows. Inverted pleats emphasize the graceful scalloped bottom edge.

shapely valances

Performing much like wooden cornices, fabric valances top windows to lend structural interest to a gathering room, but valances yield a visually softer appearance. The fabric (a single layer or multiple layers) can be cut and sewn to permanently form a distinct shape, such as scallops *above*, or pendants. Or you can hang a rectangle of fabric so it falls loosely to form full, undulating swags and tails, as shown in the living room *opposite*. The various looks can suit almost any style, depending on the shape and fabric you choose.

THE LONG AND SHORT OF VALANCES There are no hard and fast rules declaring how long to make a valance; the choice is yours. One guideline suggests making the valance one-fifth the height of the window, but you can adjust the measurement as desired. To avoid making a costly mistake with decorator fabric when making your own valance, first create a muslin test pattern. Hang the muslin and adjust the length to get the right look. Then use the muslin as a template for cutting your fabric.

tailoredtoppers

"Clean and simple" best describes valances that communicate crisp style by shunning fussy details. Tailored valances employ straight lines and sometimes unpretentious pleats to top a window with understated, yet sophisticated, elegance. Use a tailored valance alone or pair it with matching panels, as shown *above*, or with panels fashioned from another material, such as those *opposite*, for more coverage, color, and pattern.

VALANCE PLACEMENT You don't have to mount a valance right at the window trim. Place it higher—generally 2 to 5 inches above the molding—so more light enters and the window appears grander.

❶ Though this floral-pattern valance features triple pleats, the box style is straight and uncomplicated, matching the straightforward attitude of the furnishings. The topper is mounted just under the crown molding, helping to flood the room with light and enhance the sunny effects of the yellow in the drapery fabric and on the walls.

❷ A simple, tailored valance gives this living room a fresh take on 1930s elegance. Neatly fashioned from striped silk taffeta, the valance pairs with lace panels to permit soft light to filter into the room, which is furnished with elegant velvet cutwork and brocade upholstered pieces.

sheerwill

Sheers no longer have to hide beneath heavier draperies—though they're beautiful when layered with other window treatments to provide privacy and interest. (For instance, the cotton valance layered with the white sheer *above center* brings soft dimension to a gathering room, while two layers of sheers lend depth to the window treatments *above right*.) Sheers are now also prized for their breezy look when used alone to gently filter sunlight without darkening a room. Available in an array of colors, such as the lavender panels *above left*, sheers also come in prints with barely-there tone-on-tone motifs.

① Muted lavender sheers soften the appearance of dark bamboo blinds, which are lowered for privacy and light control when it's time to nap on the antique chaise. When the blinds are raised, the feather-light wisps of fabric beckon the essence of the outdoors to come inside.

② A patterned fabric valance tops airy white sheers to draw the eye upward. The strokes of bright color repeat a note of cottage charm established by the weather-worn coffee table. The valance also brings visual weight to the sheers, and the beaded fringe provides a flirty finish.

③ Sheers come in patterns too: A pocket-weave sheer fabric made of ivory-color cotton and lime green-hued polyester forms these checkerboard-pattern drapery panels. The look is fresh and hip to suit the acrylic coffee table and casual sink-in-soft sofa.

Although tab-top curtains most often dress windows in casual and contemporary spaces, the look is versatile enough to suit traditional styles too. The secret lies in your choice of fabric and the design of the tabs themselves. Velvet, for example, sends a more serious, sumptuous message, while cotton chintz yields a lighter, cheerful attitude to complement a cottage, such as the treatments *below right*. Clean-lined, tailored tabs make sense in a modern space, while tabs embellished with embossed brass buttons lend elegance to a traditional living room. Because the curtain rod is visible between the tabs, select a decorative model that provides an attractive backdrop for the tabs. For variety, skip the rod and slip the tabs over individual hooks or knobs secured to the wall above the window, as in the treatment shown on *page 64*.

TAB DETERMINATION Factor in the height of the tabs when you determine where to hang a curtain rod. Also keep in mind what can be seen between the tabs; select an attractive rod, hooks, or knobs because any of these will be at least partially visible. Window trim may also be on view and should complement the fabric.

*keeping*tabs

1

2

① Tabs made of checked fabric and secured with handmade clay buttons serve as charming dressmaker details that cap off these golden toile panels—ideal for a cottage-style setting. Ending the panels at the windowsill keeps the look relaxed.

② It's possible to add romance to an ordinary tab-top curtain: Layer floral-pattern sheer panels over a straightforward striped fabric. Clip-on rings slip over each tab to grasp the top edge of the sheers and hold them in place.

③ A black wrought-iron rod is a smart choice for a room with French flair, so why conceal it? Floor-to-ceiling striped taffeta panels feature matching tabs that keep the rod partially in view. A smocked header also helps lure the eye to the hardware.

❶ Tall windows play an important role in making this great-room sunny and allowing the outdoors inside. Wood blinds suit the connection of the space with nature, providing light control without detracting from the view.

❷ Pairing wood blinds with plush draperies in this sitting room keeps the look elegant and formal. The wall-to-wall drapery panels, finished with inverted pleats, are mounted at the ceiling. Fabric treatments such as these can conceal blinds when they are drawn up to the top of the window.

Consider blinds the chameleons of the window treatment world: Their clean-lined design works with virtually any style of room, a bonus if you like to regularly change the look of a room by hanging different fabric panels or valances. You can mount blinds alone, as in the space *left*, or pair them with panels (as shown *below*), valances, or cornices. Use blinds when you desire the ultimate control of light and privacy; the slats tilt to allow varying degrees of sunlight and privacy or can close completely. Pull a cord to draw a blind up to the top of the window, allowing unencumbered light and views. Blinds are available in an array of materials, including wood, faux wood, and vinyl and can be painted to match any decor.

blindambition

1

2

Add a little razzle-dazzle to a fabric panel or valance in your living, family, or great-room by selecting from a vast sea of embellishments. Visit crafts and fabrics stores to find buttons, braids, bows, ribbon, fringe, cords, and trinkets (even nailheads, as shown *opposite*) that you can stitch or glue into place. Adornments such as these are an ideal way to dress up custom-made or plain, purchased window treatments.

*embellished*strategies

1 Jute bouillon fringe along the edge of these khaki-and-blue striped panels adds texture that contrasts nicely with the woven bamboo shade. Adding to the substantial look of these panels are the chunky wooden rings threaded onto the beefy rods.

2 Window treatments allow you to experiment with unusual juxtapositions of casual and formal fabrics and embellishments. Upholstery nailheads are used on this window treatment and some of the furnishings. The nailheads emphasize the crisp Italian pleats and casual white cotton border that top off these formal pomegranate-pattern damask draperies.

❶ Roman shades, which can be drawn up to the tops of the windows, ensure wide-angle views of a meadow and woods from this sunny dining room. Fashioned from buttery yellow fabric, the shades blend seamlessly with the walls to create an uninterrupted look that doesn't detract from the view.
❷ This casual dining area offers the best view from the house of the bay beyond. Because privacy isn't a concern, the neutral-hued linen panels are purely decorative—meant only to frame and soften the magnificent scene.

● **ON PAGE 28** A sunny breakfast alcove is a fitting location for the casual character of these tie-up shades. In this case, the shades pair with clean, white panels to enhance the light and airy look of the room. To learn more about tie-up shades, turn to *page 11*.

1

2

① Call it dressed-down regality. This formal dining room—with its crisp white wainscoting, elegant floral wallcovering, and high ceiling—takes on a more casual attitude with the addition of red-and-white plaid panels. A full swag with fringe is a nod to the formal heritage of the room.

② Sumptuous silk panels feature a tone-on-tone plaid that relaxes the look of this elegant fabric. For luxury, the treatment puddles on the floor and features an embroidered edge with fringe. The look is sophisticated but not too serious. The creative use of tiebacks also makes this a clever solution for arched windows.

plaidplays

If you thought that plaid fabrics were for kids' bedrooms only, you'll be delighted to see how gracious plaid can be in a dining room—creating an atmosphere where sophistication and comfort coexist. The secret is to use generous amounts of fabric to create full, voluptuous panels and swags that communicate elegance. The result is a look that's relaxed yet luxurious. Similarly, the type of fabric you select can present plaid in a whole new light. Silk panels, like those shown *opposite*, seem fitting in a high-style sitting room with a dining spot. Keep in mind that tone-on-tone plaids or plaids in one color plus white work best to preserve a formal attitude. If you want a more casual look, select plaids in smaller scales featuring two or more colors.

❶ A small dining room makes a big statement when dressed in three clean shades: yellow, white, and magenta. Horizontal stripes painted on the walls create the illusion of a larger space, while wood shutters and matelassé panels convey a sense of comfort. The simple wrought-iron rod introduces a pleasing textural touch.

❷ A warm maize color on the walls casts a cozy character in this large dining room with a high ceiling. Substantial moldings and woodwork dressed in white stand out as an impressive frame for a breezy stationary shade fashioned from honey-tone linen and outlined in silk cording. A sweeping swag at the top of the shade and a tassel dangling from the bottom serve as regal finishing flourishes.

When you want to dine or cook in a space that always feels cheerful and bright—even if the room is on the north side of the house—use window treatments and walls together to create a lively look. Yellow is the color you can always count on to convey a sunny feel. Use it lavishly via paint and fabrics to infuse a room with year-round sunshine. In both these dining rooms, yellow teams with crisp white to give the eyes a resting place and offer an appealing counterpoint to the glowing color. If you are planning an all-yellow dining room, use more than one shade; employing several hues—from the deepest gold to the palest cream—adds interest to a monochromatic palette.

*glowing*reviews

The sink may be the most utilitarian spot in the kitchen, but that doesn't mean you should employ a dowdy above-the-sink window treatment. In fact, dish duty might fly by a little faster if you dress this window on your world with style that stokes your spirit.

To preserve privacy and block intense sunlight, select a versatile Roman shade, such as the one *below left*. If these needs aren't high on your list—but watching the kids playing in the yard is—top the window with a valance, such as those *below center* and *below right*, which won't obstruct the view. No matter the style of the treatment you choose, pattern and color can play a primary design role above the sink. Select hues and a motif that pull all the elements of your kitchen together in this one key location.

highintentions

❶ The renovated kitchen in this 1930s house earns an updated look with a shimmery fumed-copper backsplash and gleaming stainless-steel fixtures. A clean-lined Roman shade above the sink suits the new, more contemporary elements; the leaf-and-vine pattern echoes colors from the backsplash, the walls, and the outdoors.

❷ In a kitchen with cottage sensibilities, a tab-top valance in yellow-and-white plaid above the sink (and below the sink as a sweet cover-up) suits the unpretentious setting.

❸ This kitchen successfully balances dark cabinetry and counters with neutral walls and sunlight. The rooster-motif valance above the sink visually links all the elements. The swagged folds were planned to give the motif maximum visibility.

2 3

❶ Though cafés are petite in size, they can make a big statement. These panels—made from a whimsical fabric and trimmed with bands of solid-color fabric—casually dangle from rings that are attached to the back of the fabric with drapery pins. Buttons glued to the sides of the pinch pleats add playful details.

❷ These cotton muslin café curtains are embroidered with words in neutral-tone threads. You can have an embroidery shop embellish your fabric if you don't have a sewing machine that is properly equipped. You can also add words using iron-on transfers or create them with fabric paint and stencils.

Café curtains typically cover the bottom half of a window and are usually paired with a valance. The popular treatment provides privacy with a view and fashionably dresses a window without full-length attire. Where cafés start and stop is your choice. Hanging a curtain rod parallel to the middle sash is most common. For windows with deep sills, such as the one *opposite*, hem the curtains to stop just above so the panels don't flare outward.

*charming*cafés

baybeauties

Consider yourself fortunate if you have a kitchen or dining area with a bay window that drinks in sunlight and views. To avoid concealing these assets, select a minimally sized treatment, such as the valances *above* and *opposite*. Dressmaker details—such as bows and pleats—can further promote the focal-point status of the window. If your bay window faces the street, add café panels for privacy (see *pages 38* and *39*).

1 Though small, an apple green-hued valance makes a big statement at this kitchen bay window. Yellow bows, piping, and tiny checked gimp along the hem give the valance a sassy style.

2 A tailored toile valance makes the large bay window in this breakfast area more cozy yet doesn't impede on the window seat. The fabric used in the valance is repeated within the room to enhance the balance of casual and formal.

❶ Luxurious draperies in subtle colors exemplify an interplay of casual and refined in this dining room; the masterful mix of hand-embroidered linen and playful gingham (for the lining) are the secret to this dual-personality treatment. The swag and jabots, whose colors are derived from the fabric on the chairs, are detailed with pencil pleats, cording, and fringe trim that give the treatment more interest and style.

❷ The sunny disposition of this dining area is enhanced by moiré swags and long, crisply pleated jabots. Closely matching the fabric to the yellow walls creates a unified appearance. Cream-color lining on the jabots—visible in the cascades—adds understated interest.

elegantjabots

Jabots-and-swag window treatments, which feature a swooping swag flanked by narrow pleated panels called jabots, are the hallmark of stately dining rooms. If this formal look appeals to you, choose a medium-weight or lightweight fabric that drapes well to achieve the full semi-circle of a swag and the gently cascading effect desired for the jabots. For extra opulence, add fringe, as shown *opposite*, or beaded trim. Because the ends of jabots are typically pleated at opposing angles, they offer an ideal opportunity to introduce a coordinating lining fabric.

Whether you want to hide unattractive hanging hardware or introduce architecture in a low-key kitchen or dining room, you can achieve your goal with a shapely cornice or valance. Use a window-topping element alone or pair it with cafés or panels for even more dimension. A cornice can be wrapped with batting and fabric for a plush, upholstered appearance *below left*, constructed of wood and painted similar to the example *below center*, or composed of a mix of materials, such as the unique glass-and-wood version *below right*.

well-formedsolutions

❶ Dark-tone, visually heavy antique furnishings in this dining room appear less austere thanks to a fabric-wrapped cornice and breezy panels. The leaf-and-plaid pattern damask fabric lends a contemporary twist to the traditional space. Plaid trim softens the stark contrast between the stationary white linen side panels and the caramel-and-beige color cornice, and casual tassels add a touch of playfulness. The gentle arch along the bottom edge of the cornice allows in as much light as possible.

❷ Install a shapely cornice to throw curves into a kitchen composed of straight lines. The wood cutout of this cornice creates a distinctive outline; the hand-painted plaid design in bold red and white draws further attention to the cornice. To soften the treatment, "shirred" areas give the effect of a more free-flowing valance. Cafés below filter light and offer privacy when pulled across the windows.

❸ A leaded-glass "cornice" provides a crowning touch above the pass-through window from the kitchen to a sunporch, adding character to both rooms—a good lesson that even interior windows can benefit from treatments.

2 3

❶ Pair shutters with fabric panels to soften the look and add color. These window treatments play up the casual chic atmosphere in this dining room by combining the relaxed textural qualities of woven blinds and wooden shutters. Locating the rod high on the wall makes the windows appear taller and grander.

When it comes to communicating style, interior wood shutters are some of the most versatile treatments in the window world. Their simple design allows them to fit unobtrusively with styles ranging from traditional to contemporary.

Install shutters for stand-alone style, as shown *below*, or pair them with other window treatments, such as woven blinds, to bring textural interest to windows and to enhance a particular look. You can also layer shutters with fabric. For example, pair café shutters on the lower half of a window with a valance above for casual appeal. Or dress up bifold shutters with woven blinds and floor-to-ceiling panels, as shown *left*.

Shutters in white and wood tones are common, but you have other options: You can prime and paint shutters to complement any scheme.

shuttersavvy

1

❷ The louvers that comprise these plantation-style shutters open at various angles to regulate the amount of light coming in during the day. Their easy operation allows items displayed on the wide window ledge to remain undisturbed. In addition, the uncomplicated design of the shutters doesn't compete with the chandelier and furnishings.

2

Windows open your home to the outside world, but sometimes they deliver too much of a good thing. Bright, warm shafts of light can ward off winter doldrums, but they can also bring in glare and furniture-fading rays. And, although views are wonderful when you want to look outside, there are times when you don't want anyone peering inside, such as when dining at a banquette (such as the cozy example *below*). Shades offer the ideal solution when you want to control light and views; depending on the material you choose, they can adapt to any style.

coolshades

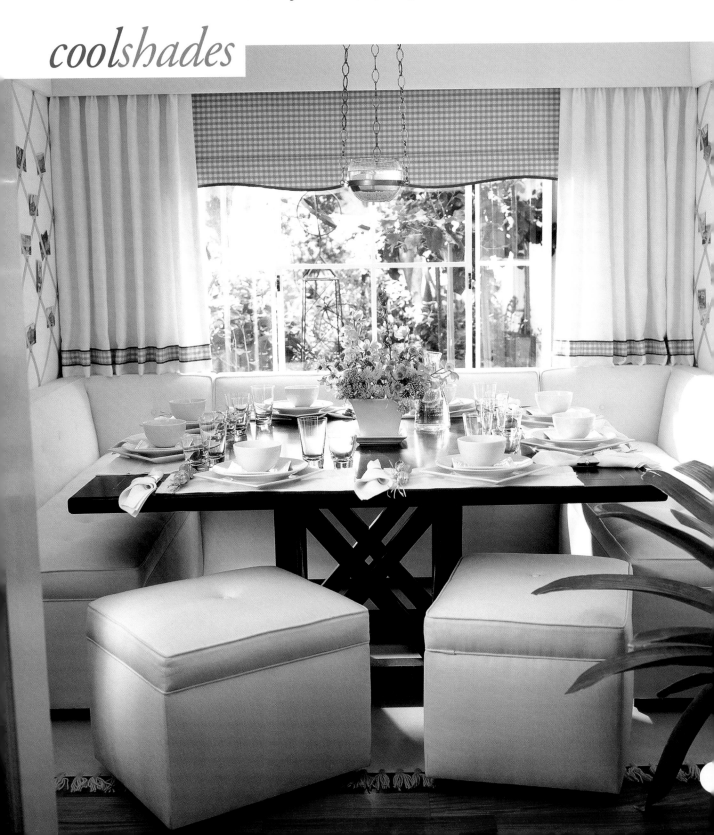

❶ A gingham shade combines with white linen panels, trimmed in matching gingham, to make this window treatment both sweet and sophisticated. A scalloped edge on the shade introduces a softening element and offers a practical handle for pulling down the shade when privacy or light control is needed.

❷ Toile Roman shades offer light control for these kitchen greenhouse windows, but they also provide pleasing pattern and softness when drawn up to reveal the view.

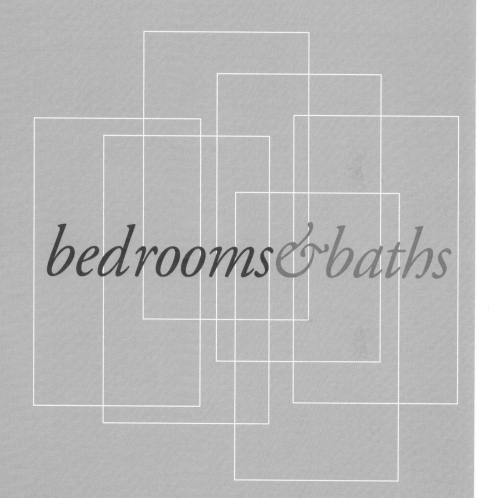

bedrooms&baths

1 A group of windows in this bathroom allows in ample natural light. Selecting blinds—rather than draperies—ensures the sunny purpose of the windows is unhindered. Because the blinds mount inside the window frames, wallcoverings and window trim remain uninterrupted.

ON PAGE 50 Morning light is a wonderful thing—unless, of course, you're trying to sleep in. Shutters have operable slats that tilt to let in varying amounts of sunlight. Slats also close to provide privacy and block light.

relax&refresh

Bedrooms and bathrooms are places reserved for rest and rejuvenation. Select window treatment styles and fabrics that reflect a sense of refuge, keeping in mind how much privacy you need. The ideas in this chapter—an exciting assortment for adult and children's bedrooms and baths— show how you can capture the look, feel, and function you want in these personal spaces.

light & privacy When privacy and light control are your primary concerns in the bedroom and bathroom, dress windows with interior wood shutters, such as the ones in the bedroom on *page 50*, or blinds, such as those in the bathroom *left*. Shutters feature louvers that can be opened to fully admit light and views, closed for privacy and insulation, or adjusted at a range of angles in between to allow in varying amounts of sunlight. Shutters mounted on operative hinges can swing open, but they may infringe on the space if not installed to lie flat against flanking walls when open. Blinds have slats that function much the same as louvers. The primary difference between shutters and blinds is that you can pull a cord to raise a blind to the top of the window to completely open the space to light and views.

shadeseekers

Curtains typically get the glory for their full coverage and abundance of color, pattern, and texture, but shades combine pragmatism with style—providing privacy, light control, and a full complement of color and pattern when closed. When you draw the shade up to let the world in, you minimize the fabric presence; yet the shade still lends a softening effect to the hard lines of trim and windowpanes. You'll be amazed by the wide variety of styles to which shades can adapt, such as the casual appeal of the loosely designed ivory Roman shade *above left*, or the French flair of the scallop-edged version *above right*.

❶ Roman shades hang loosely to enhance a feeling of tranquility. The tone-on-tone ivory striped shades in this bathroom provide privacy for daytime bathing without blocking natural light. When drawn upward, the shades form folds that are full, rounded, and curved slightly downward—not a stiff crease in sight. The effect agrees wholeheartedly with the soothing atmosphere created by the monochromatic color scheme.

❷ Although the pleats on this Roman shade are crisp, the scalloped edge and floral striped fabric make it casual. The design, with its textured trim and fancy, curving silhouette, is a nod to French styling.

❸ Pleated or honeycomb shades, such as these, come in light-filtering and light-blocking versions; make your choice depending on how much privacy you desire. A honeycomb, or cellular, shade features two layers of fabric that fold in opposite directions, providing additional insulation and increased protection from ultraviolet rays of the sun. Shades such as these can also be installed to rise up from the bottom of the windowsill to allow privacy for the lower portion of the window with a partial view above the shade.

*great*shades

Shades can also be very clean-lined and contemporary in appearance, such as the one in the bedroom *above left*. If you want an uncomplicated treatment but prefer a little more design oomph, select subtly patterned fabrics for your shade and add a simple adornment, such as the concentric circles motif on the tasseled shade *above right* and the fringed scarflike valance on the bathroom shades *opposite*.

❶ This bedroom is all about the lovely wall treatments—the paneled wainscoting and the delicate floral painting on the wall above—so the window treatment needs to play a secondary role. A simply designed, inside-mount shade—one that hangs within the window frame—lets the surrounding trim and wainscoting remain uninterrupted.

❷ This window is the first thing the owners see upon entering the little bathroom, so the treatment needs to be a special focal point—without being overbearing. Still, privacy is a concern, as is preserving a distant ocean view. A pair of stationary treatments fashioned from swirl-pattern white organza provides the solution. On the upper half of the window, the treatment mimics the look of a Roman shade but is inoperative. On the lower portion of the window, a wooden frame is covered with a layer of muslin and topped with organza. The fabrics are wrapped to the back of the frame edges and stapled in place. Decorative cording is glued to the edges, and a glass doorknob and tassel finish the frame.

❸ Ornate lighting fixtures, built-in storage, beaded-board wainscoting, and brass-finish faucets work together to give this bathroom vintage flavor with a hint of Victorian elegance. Selecting unpretentious white Roman shades for the trio of tall windows lets the other features stand out. Adorning the shades with a triangular scarf-style valance with black fringe nods to the 1800s styling of the bath without making a fuss.

The bedroom and bath are the perfect places for the romantic, billowy effect that balloon shades convey. Balloons also provide the fabric abundance of draperies with the privacy of shades. When raised, a balloon shade will cover one-third to one-half of the window. When choosing fabrics for balloon shades, keep in mind that the gathers make patterns tough to distinguish. Select solids or patterns with a small overall print, or plan so the pattern repeat falls on each "balloon" and is visible—rather than hidden in the creases.

beautifulballoons

❶ This sumptuous balloon shade features cascading scallops that culminate in graceful, blousy folds along the bottom edge. Cords strung through rings on the back make the shade movable; as the treatment is raised, the vertical gathers create dramatic poufs.

❷ This luxurious golden-and-taupe striped silk balloon shade complements the wall treatment and serves as the focal point of the narrow bathroom. To keep the poufs intact, a balloon shade often remains raised to serve as a valance, as shown here. In this case, the balloon teams with bifold shutters to address privacy needs.

*tranquil*treatments

Floor-length panels can proclaim, "Hey, look at me!" when composed of bright colors or dramatic patterns. Or they can whisper quietly when simply designed and subtly hued—an ideal approach if you dream of a serene refuge from the world. To capture a calm look, use fabrics in soft colors, as shown *above*, or lavish a window in pristine white like the panels *opposite*.

❶ Lush cotton-duck, tab-top panels puddle on the floor to voluptuously frame the garden view seen from this soaking tub. When breezes pass through the open windows, the curtains billow romantically, emphasizing the calming influence of white and making this bathroom seem all the more serene.

❷ A bird-watching theme, established with blue-and-taupe aviary fabric, soothes this former sleeping porch of a 1900s house. To avoid concealing the architectural beauty of the windows, the walls are dressed instead. Floor-to-ceiling panels hang between, rather than over, the windows, lending a soft, cocoonlike feel to the space. An ironsmith hand-forged the iron curtain rods and bird-silhouette brackets. The draperies hang from metal rings just inches from the 9-foot-tall ceiling.

chintzcharm

Invite the refreshing appeal of an English garden into your bedroom or bath using treatments fashioned from the flowery, romantic fabric known as chintz. First popularized in the early 17th century when European explorers brought back richly colored fabrics adorned with flower or bird motifs from India, chintz has become a decorating mainstay. The close-knit patterns create an atmosphere that is upbeat and warm and suitable for almost any type of treatment. To update the look, some old patterns have received new color palettes, such as the vivid scheme *left* and *below*. You can use chintz alone or mix it with other fabrics to create a cozy feel for a bedroom, as shown *opposite*.

1

2

3

❶ Chintz draperies—full gathered panels topped with tailored handkerchief valances—inspired hues for the upholstery in this bedroom sitting area. Bright spots of solid color—a chartreuse cricket table and a curvilinear candy-apple red lamp—also echo hues found in the treatments. Drapery rods are placed high on the wall to exaggerate the height of the room and close to the wall to emphasize the under-the-eaves atmosphere.
❷ Love the look of chintz but not a low-key color palette? You can find updated chintz fabrics: The curtain fabrics in the adjoining bedroom sitting area and bathroom are historically accurate patterns that have been recolorized with modern hues. Stationary drapery panels continue

the look from the sitting area and soften the arched, tile-lined bathtub niche. A flat-panel Roman shade dresses the window in a simple style similar to the panels adorning the bathtub niche.
❸ An abundance of windows and doors in this bedroom cultivated a design that brings flowers and greenery inside. The cheerful yellow, green, and red palette comes from the chintz draped lavishly on the bed. For a cozier look, the chintz pairs with plaid at the windows, where the middle "scoop" of the valance brings the chintz center stage. Designed to showcase the pattern of the fabric, the upper walls of the bedroom sport light-tone damask wallpaper.

accentgems

Even the smallest bedroom can sparkle with style: Introduce a few unexpected features to take the focus off the square footage and on your great taste. One way is to use unique window treatment hardware, such as the glass knobs *above* or unusual tiebacks. You can also dress up plain draperies with purchased embellishments, such as cording, fringe, or tassels, or play up a color theme by custom-painting fabric or drapery rings to suit the decor, as in this bedroom *opposite*.

❶ You can repurpose items to function as drapery hangers. These silk-trimmed dotted sheers loosely drape from crystal doorknobs, which are anchored to the drywall with double-sided screws.

❷ Silky fabrics for the windows and bed and silver-leaf grass cloth for the walls give this room a serene feel. To complement the fabrics, the drapery rings are painted a shimmery silver. The drapery rod is covered with the striped fabric used for the duvet; continuing the pattern from the bed to the windows creates visual balance.

❶ Orange is an especially popular hue today, and this room takes on the happy hue with gusto. White linen draperies at the window balance the abundance of orange in this bedroom but continue the theme with orange edging and smart orange button accents across the header. A lacy orange bed canopy, embellished with orange-dyed satin ribbon, hangs from bamboo poles that are suspended from the ceiling by monofilament thread. The bed coverlet and neckroll are fashioned from orange fabric that features the same pattern as the canopy.

❷ Purple is a perennial favorite among young people. Pairing the hue with touches of black as well as more sophisticated floral patterns at the windows and stripes on the seats gives this room a timeless appeal that will allow it to grow for many years with the occupant.

Teenagers' tastes can change as fast as their shoe sizes. That's why it's smart to choose window treatments with staying power for their bedrooms and baths. Select classic fabrics in current colors, such as the crisp white panels trimmed in orange for the bedroom *opposite*, or the bold combination of florals at the windows in the bedroom *below.* Use decorative pillows, area rugs, bed linens and coverlets, and paint to put a little changeable flair into the space.

teenretreats

The window and wall treatments you choose for your child's bedroom will determine how well the room adapts through the years. These two bedrooms offer different looks, but both promise design longevity. The green-and-red toile wallcovering paired with green-and-white gingham valance *below*, for example, are both updated classics. It's a look that can grow from toddler through the teen years. And although the bedroom *opposite* is especially playful with its larger-than-life motifs and accents, the soft sheers at the window and colorful quilt on the bed can easily transition as the occupant ages. Even the oversize painted wall flowers might tantalize a teen.

*graceful*aging

2

3

❶ Walls of curtains transform this long, narrow space in a historical house into a cozy porch with an updated look. To protect the decorative fabric dressing the screened windows, the panels are treated with fabric protector. Dressing the windows entirely in the botanical fabric would have been too expensive. Instead, the print is used to band the bottom third of each cotton duck drapery.

❷ Striking yellow walls make the most of this sunny alcove, and the tie-up shades ensure that the windows join the party. The gingham-and-vine pattern fabric and gingham ribbon ties add a big dose of cottage sweetness—a style cue carried out in white-painted furnishings and a pitcher of fresh tulips.

❸ For an upper-level sunroom, tropical-tone fabrics and accessories play up the treetop view and keep the look light and breezy. A botanical-motif fabric dominates the valances, then repeats below on pillows that grace vintage porch furniture upholstered and skirted in a linen-tone indoor-outdoor fabric (see "Fabrics for the Elements" *opposite*). Gauzy panels casually clipped to wrought-iron café rods provide privacy along the bottom half of the windows.

Positioning a built-in or freestanding bench in front of a window is all about settling in to enjoy the view or to relax and read. Choose window treatments that make the most of those activities, such as the awning treatment *opposite bottom* that makes it easy to see outside, or the sill-length panels *below* that don't get in the way of lounging. You can harmonize the cushion and the window coverings with coordinating fabrics or create a homey, casual mix of two or more distinct patterns. The bay window *below*, for example, is more inviting with the mini plaid on the bench and toile-pattern panels at the windows. In lieu of fabrics, you can focus on textural options, such as the shutters and matchstick blinds *opposite top*.

*window*seats

❶ A long bench follows the curve of this grand bay window, providing a place to relax and enjoy a beautiful view. Dressing the seat is a tailored blue-on-blue mini-plaid skirt that mimics the bold wallpaper and balances the wavy lines of the scalloped valance above. Toile drapery panels, hemmed just shy of the seat, break up the many vertical and horizontal lines of the tonal plaids while introducing yellow—a favorite companion of blue. Matchstick blinds peek out from behind the valance and offer privacy when needed. Tiebacks made from the same fabrics as the pillows and embellished with a small bow do their job with a delicate touch.

❷ An antique settee steps in as a window seat in this room. Because the house already features louvered interior doors, employing shutters at the window was a natural design decision. Bifold shutters fold open and out of the way so that anyone seated can lean back and soak up the sun. Matchstick blinds above the shutters lend visual interest and provide privacy when lowered.

❸ Located in a side entry, this window seat makes a great first impression. A cheerful, fruity fabric and an unusual awning-style valance draw attention to the window. The awning preserves the view and creates a charming "indoor café" atmosphere. The tailored treatment is fashioned over a wooden frame. The fabric was sewn together in sections with the scalloped edge, lined with a coordinating stripe that also appears on the cushion, and then stapled and glued to the frame. Cording decoratively finishes the seams.

1

2

3

framedcomfort

The fabrics and style of the treatments you choose for a window seat can communicate a look that is light and airy, as do the sheer draperies *opposite*, or can create a cozy, cocoonlike setting, as shown *above*, where weighty panels and a substantial valance frame a window seat nook. Either way, outfitting your window seat from top to bottom will elevate it to focal-point status.

❶ A French-style table and chairs encouraged an elegant treatment for this dining room window seat. Toile, a classic French fabric beloved for its pastoral scenes, is the perfect choice for the panels and valance. Plaid—another timeless pattern—pairs with the toile as edging to relax the look, but puddling the panels on the floor prevents the treatment from appearing too casual. Tasseled trim outlines the panels and accentuates the points on the inverted-pleat valance for a graceful finish. A simple lace panel hangs beneath the draperies as a complementary old-world accent.

❷ For this bedroom window seat, creating a sense of charm and romance began with a soft blush-color cushion and piles of ivory, cream, and blush pillows. The grand expanse of glass behind this seat features a billowy series of cotton lace swags shirred on a custom-arched rod, as well as a pair of narrow side draperies attached to the rod with fabric rosettes. Ball fringe adds a jaunty finish.

Your window seat can feel like a mini retreat—a cozy escape right there in the room it occupies. It's a goal you can achieve whether your favorite style is country *below*, cottage, traditional, contemporary *opposite*, or somewhere in between. Using plump pillows and a thick, inviting cushion in combination with functional and fabulous window treatments is the key to success.

LINING FOR COMFORT To increase your comfort level at a window seat, or any window, choose from basic, blackout, or thermal lining for the fabric panels or shades. Basic lining—usually made of tightly woven cotton or cotton-blend fabric in white or off-white—provides minimal protection from sun damage. To ensure that virtually no rays penetrate, use blackout lining, which features a thick, gray coating on one side. If warmth at a cold window is your goal, add thermal lining, which features a special coating that minimizes the passage of air. Thermal lining is typically available in white.

*instant*hideaways

2

❶ A daybed slides in beneath this window to serve as a seat by day and a bed for guests by night. A simple off-white Roman shade draws up to offer views and sunlight and closes when privacy is needed. Gingham panels in the foreground make this niche a cozy respite from the daily grind.

❷ Though shutters hail from an earlier era, their simple design suits them to any number of room styles, including this pristine, contemporary living room. Folding back the lower shutters during the day allows full access to the seats. At night, with the shutters and louvers tightly closed, these window treatments offer some insulative value.

Of all the "special" spaces, the hallway may be the most easily forgotten because it is a place you pass through but rarely linger in. Turn a languishing liability into a decorative asset by giving these typically small areas big style. The green-and-cream checked cornice with complementary side panels *opposite* shows just how dramatic you can go. You can also use window treatments and wallcoverings in the hallway to smooth transitions between rooms. The cream-color draperies on the French door *below*, for example, feature black-and-taupe plaid trim to tie in with the black-and-white toile that extends up the staircase.

hallways

❶ To give a bland hallway an elegant touch, these tall, narrow French doors feature airy panels with a ruffled header. The treatments hang from swing-arm rods that swoosh the panels out of the way when the doors open. To prevent the panels from catching in the doors, loops stitched to the inner edge of each panel slip over cup hooks attached to the trim.

❷ A walkway between a bedroom and bath becomes an intimate dressing retreat thanks to elegant furnishings and a window treatment. Gridlike panels on the closet doors inspired the checked cornice. The cornice and panels are made from faux suede for velvety texture. Jumbo brown faux-suede welting defines the squares on the cornice.

homeoffices

Whether you spend 40 hours or 40 minutes in your home office every week, make it a fun, attractive place to be. Choose comfortable furnishings and wrap the space with stylish walls and windows. The office *above*, for example, uses toile to toss in a note of tradition with the more contemporary lines of the Parsons-style desk. If your office is small, keep the window treatments streamlined, like the shades in the cozy niche *opposite right*. Because almost every home office now has a computer, your treatments may need to cut glare—the primary purpose of the panels *opposite left*, which work in layers to create a tranquil mood.

❶ You can make a small office feel cozy, but not cramped, by treating the walls and windows with the same fabric. Pinch-pleated panels of brown-and-cream toile in a whimsical garden motif cover these walls and continue to the window as curtains hung from a bamboo pole. Natural linen fabric fashions light-filtering shades secured with grosgrain ribbon. For a fun finish to this hardworking space, binder clips pinch the fabric pleats, and paper clips trim the curtain tiebacks.

❷ In this home office, a double layer of semitransparent fabric and an innovative design create a practical, pretty solution to the problem of computer glare. Crisp, white linen stationary panels installed inside the window frame ensure that the elegant trim isn't covered. The panels are mounted on tension rods at the top and bottom of the window. A narrower sheer panel hung from a steel swing-arm rod is layered in front for an updated take on an old-fashioned concept (swing-arm rods were popular in the early 1900s).

❸ If you carve an office out of a slice of space, you'll want to make the area feel as open as possible. This office, for example, fits in over a third-floor stairwell. The trio of windows fills the niche with sunlight; using simple shades allows light control while keeping the look clean and uncluttered.

*home*theaters

In a home theater, light control ranks at the top of the list of needs—along with state-of-the-art electronics. After all, what's the use of owning a top-quality television if you can't see the screen clearly during the day due to sunlight glare? In the city, light control can be an issue at night as well. Select opaque fabrics, such as the treatment in the theater room *above* and *opposite*. Or purchase light-blocking shades or hard treatments, such as shutters. Light-blocking lining added to the back of a fabric window treatment (see *page 82*) can also prevent sunlight from ruining the show.

AUTOMATED MAGIC Imagine eliminating the cords hanging from your window treatments. Motorized operating systems are now available for Roman shades, roller shades, and draperies. The systems can open and close your window treatments (or adjust them somewhere in between) at the touch of a button on a remote control. Some motorized systems can also be programmed to operate at preset times—to open at dawn and close at dusk, for example. The systems can also control multiple windows at one time—no more running around the house to open and close the draperies.

❶ In a theater room with a wide doorway, you'll need an additional means for controlling light. In this case, opaque curtain panels can be drawn across the opening to block light that spills in from the adjoining rec room.

❷ Flipping a switch lowers the light-blocking window treatment in this lower-level theater room. A wood valance hides the motorized mechanisms and conceals the blackout shade when it's raised.

decorating *pantry*

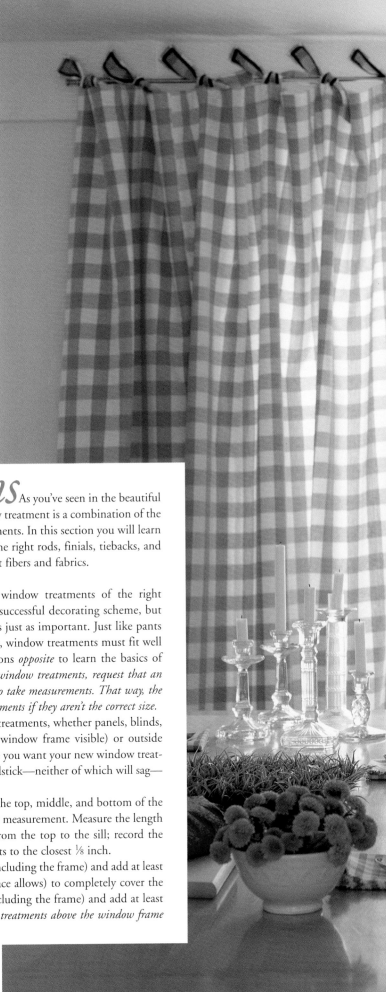

choices&decisions

As you've seen in the beautiful spaces throughout this book, a successful window treatment is a combination of the right style, size, fabric, hardware, and embellishments. In this section you will learn how to measure window treatments and select the right rods, finials, tiebacks, and other decorative elements. You'll also learn about fibers and fabrics.

measuring success

Finding window treatments of the right style, color, and fabric is crucial to achieving a successful decorating scheme, but selecting the perfect size of window treatment is just as important. Just like pants of the right length can make an outfit look chic, window treatments must fit well to be an asset to your room. Use the illustrations *opposite* to learn the basics of measuring windows. *Note: If you order custom window treatments, request that an associate from the workroom come to your home to take measurements. That way, the company will be responsible for replacing the treatments if they aren't the correct size.*

You have two options for hanging window treatments, whether panels, blinds, shutters, or shades: inside mount (leaving the window frame visible) or outside mount (covering the frame). Regardless of where you want your new window treatments to hang, use a steel measuring tape or yardstick—neither of which will sag—to ensure accurate measurements.

■ **INSIDE MOUNT** Measure the opening width at the top, middle, and bottom of the window (inside the frame); record the narrowest measurement. Measure the length of the window at the left, middle, and right, from the top to the sill; record the longest measurement. Round your measurements to the closest 1/8 inch.

■ **OUTSIDE MOUNT** Measure the window width (including the frame) and add at least 3 inches to each side of the opening (if wall space allows) to completely cover the window frame. Measure the window length (including the frame) and add at least 2 inches for hardware. *Note: Mounting window treatments above the window frame can visually heighten a room.*

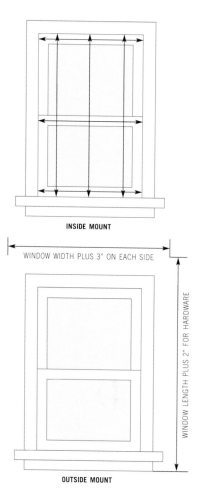

INSIDE MOUNT

WINDOW WIDTH PLUS 3" ON EACH SIDE

WINDOW LENGTH PLUS 2" FOR HARDWARE

OUTSIDE MOUNT

SIZE WISE

After you decide where you are going to mount a window treatment, determine the length of the treatment. For draperies and curtains, measure from the location of the rod to where you want the panels to fall. Consider the style of the room when choosing an appropriate length. For instance, long, flowing panels will look better in a formal living room than in a bistro-style kitchen. Also, who uses the room can influence length. Do you want your pets nesting in panels that puddle on the floor?

❶ These layered window treatments—an inside-mount shade and outside-mount panels—perfectly complement the relaxed feel of this country-inspired dining room. The oversize checked panels casually rest on the floor.

● ON PAGE 90 Long flowing panels suspended from a black wrought-iron rod can be completely drawn to the sides of this door and grand wall of windows to allow in fresh air and views of the lush yard. The shape of the finials echoes the cabinet hardware, forging a link between the elements. Use the information in this chapter to help you choose the right fabrics and hardware for any window treatment.

1

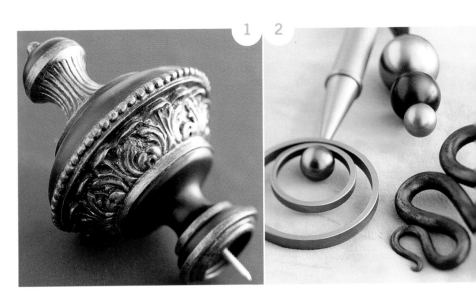

finials, trims & tiebacks
(and more ways to dress up your window treatments)

Whether you purchase ready-mades from a discount store or splurge on custom treatments, remember the details: tassels, fringe, finials, curtain clips, and more. These decorative elements, which are available at crafts stores, department stores, and home centers, accentuate even the most ordinary of panels and play up any decorating scheme. Window hardware used to be all about function; now these little extras are getting their time to shine! This section shows you various options for dressing treatments in any room of your home. Finials are shown here and on *pages 96–97*. See *pages 98–99* for tassels, trims, and rings; turn to *pages 100–101* for tiebacks.

FINIALS. Whether you prefer understated wood knobs or flashy jewel-encrusted baubles, finials add a fun finishing touch to window ensembles. Here is a look at some of the options.

FAST FINIALS
Can't find just the right finial to complement your new window treatments? Do you want a quick way to update your existing treatments? Unfinished, inexpensive wood finials are widely available at home centers and crafts stores. Personalize them quickly and easily with paint (prime first for best coverage), faux jewels (attach using hot glue), or metal leaf (follow the manufacturer's directions for application).

❶ CLASSIC. This antiqued gold-tone finial has a shape and motifs derived from Greco-Roman architecture. It would look at home in a room filled with traditional-style furniture and tailored window treatments.

❷ ORGANIC. Part space age, part natural, these finials have a futuristic look. The simple shapes and earthy tones (dark bronze and soft silver) achieve an understated, contemporary look.

3 LUSTROUS COLOR. This shiny mercury glass finial has a sheen that delights the eye. The look is current and laid-back, making it perfect for both contemporary and casual settings.

4 BEJEWELED. Whether you love spicy Moroccan designs or just want a splash of playful color, look to bold finials such as these, which sport faux jewels. Let eye-catching finials take center stage by pairing them with understated rods and curtain panels.

5 NATURAL. Resembling dewdrops hanging from curving branches, this elegant finial is covered with gold leaf and embellished with purple crystals. Ornate designs such as these look particularly stunning with breezy, sheer panels.

6 BRIGHT AND SHINY. These gleaming spheres create a sleek style that's just right for a contemporary space. The finial *right* has a collar that adds distinctive styling reminiscent of a bolt and washer.

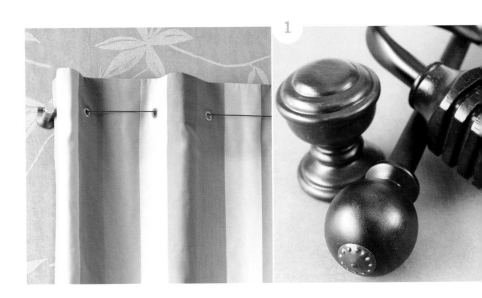

finials, trims & tiebacks

THE RIGHT ROD
From rods with brushed-metal finishes to fluted wood poles, there are myriad styles available to suit any window treatment. The following is a rundown of some of the most popular options. Before purchasing a rod—and decorative finials—measure on either side of the window to ensure there is enough space. Install hanging hardware directly into a wall stud; if this isn't possible, use an anchor rated for the total weight of your hardware and window treatment. Always ensure that walls can support the combined weight of the rod, window treatment, and any decorative embellishments.

ADJUSTABLE These curved rods—two metal pieces that fit together and can be lengthened by pulling on them—attach to mounting hardware on the wall. Inexpensive, adjustable rods aren't attractive; hence they are typically concealed by the treatment (for instance, the rod slips into a rod pocket).

CABLE WIRE Relatively new to the category are cable wires, shown *above left*, which consist of a tight silver- or gold-tone wire strung between two anchors. Depending on the mounting anchors you choose, cable wires can be mounted inside or outside a window.

METAL Available in a wide range of metals and finishes—from antique brass and pewter to chrome—metal rods are widely available at home centers and discount stores. Metal rods are typically mounted to the wall in one of two ways: Either the straight rod rests on brackets that are attached to the wall or the rod has curved ends that are attached directly to the wall.

TENSION Tension rods are "mounted" inside a window frame; they are composed of two spring-loaded metal poles that can be adjusted in length by twisting. The ends of the rods are covered with rubber tips to hold the unit in place and prevent the metal from scratching the window frame. Tension rods are typically available in a shiny or brushed-metal finish or are painted white.

UNCONVENTIONAL While it's easy to go to a store and buy ready-made rods off the rack, they aren't your only option. Use another long, thin object, such as a hockey stick or canoe paddle, to play up a design theme.

WOOD Poles made of wood can be painted—white is especially nice for cottage-style settings—stained, or left natural. Wood poles are typically fluted or smooth and rest on brackets that are attached to the wall.

① WONDERFUL WOOD. While simple wood orbs are popular choices for finials, wood can take many interesting forms. These examples have a rich finish and furniturelike details that would look handsome in a traditional setting.

② TASTE OF THE TROPICS. Top your window treatments with this grand palm finial to make every day a getaway. Look for other natural motifs, such as flowers, to bring a sense of the outside in.

③ GREAT GLASS. Glass—clear or colored—adds sparkle to a casual window treatment. The swirling effect of these finials is more interesting than smooth glass.

finials, trims & tiebacks

TRIMS, RINGS, AND TASSELS. Stock your decorating pantry with yards of colorful trims, interesting rings, and unique tassels to add design punch to any treatment. These embellishments, which can be used in conjunction with decorative rods and finials, allow you to quickly and easily change the look of your windows—seasonally or whenever the mood strikes.

Trims, such as lengths of fringe, bullion, or ribbon, are typically stitched directly to a window treatment, making them a permanent addition. However, you can attach trims to your treatments with hook-and-loop tape to swap them in a snap.

Tassels have greater versatility: You can drape them over a mounted tieback, use them to gather fabric as a tieback, hang them from a rod, or stitch them to a treatment.

Rings offer even more embellishment opportunities.

Many types of window treatments don't require rings—for instance those with tabs or a rod pocket—but if you select treatments that require a hanging device, you're in luck: From O-rings to clips, home centers and discount stores abound with options sure to suit your needs.

NO-SEW EMBELLISHMENTS
Not handy with a needle and thread but want to permanently attach trim to a treatment? Use fusible hem tape, available at fabrics stores, to secure trims with the heat of an iron.

❶ RICH WITH DETAILS. Far from ordinary, decorative rings such as these—metal embellished with fine metal rope detail and orbs—add impact along every inch of your window treatment.

❷ RIGHT RINGS. Suspend your window treatments in style with O-rings; these carved and twisted metal varieties would look especially nice in a traditional setting. O-rings are also available in plastic and wood.

❸ DOUBLE UP. Decorative tassels allow you to play up any color scheme. This oversize example—in hues of mustard, cranberry, and blue—features both heavy bullion fringe and delicate loops.

❹ TASSEL TOPPER. Tassels can be used in many ways. These richly colored examples act as finials.

3 **4**

5

6 **7**

❺ BEADED BEAUTY. Brush fringe has a lush, full appearance on its own, but add beads and baubles and the trim takes luxury to another level. If you are stitching brush fringe onto a treatment yourself, leave the stabilizing string on the bottom in place to keep the fringe tidy during handling, then remove the string after hanging the treatment.

❻ LOOPED LUXURY. Tassels are typically made of yarns, threads, and cords, but they can also be composed of fabrics, such as supple silk or soft flannel. These charming silk examples have finials with hand-painted designs—a great opportunity to play up a design motif.

❼ PICK YOUR TRIM. From simple to elaborate, trims come in many forms. From top: dainty gimp trim in reds and blues, ball fringe in eggplant, and heavy tassel trim in golden yellow.

finials, trims &tiebacks

TIEBACKS. As the name implies, tiebacks hold back drapery panels, letting in light or allowing an underlayer to be visible. Tiebacks are available in many materials and come in numerous forms, from metal shapes that attach to the wall, to fabric and cording that gather treatments. If you choose a tieback that attaches to the wall, fasten it to a wall stud because tiebacks bear some of the weight of the window treatment. If this isn't possible, install a wall anchor.

If you can't find the perfect tieback, expand your search: Many knobs and drawer pulls make stunning tiebacks. Simply use a double-headed dowel screw to attach them to the wall. You can also recruit jewelry—such as bracelets and necklaces—to serve as tiebacks.

❶ **TRADITION WITH A TWIST.** Tiebacks made of rope and cording often have a formal feeling, but when paired with a glass bauble, they take on a more casual air.

❷ **GARDEN INSPIRED.** Bring your windows into full bloom with a flower-shape tieback. This metal version would look beautiful with floral-motif curtain panels in a cottage or casual setting.

❸ **PERFECT PATINA.** These brushed-metal tiebacks have an antiqued quality that will suit nearly any decorating style. The disc has added flair thanks to a matte-finish jewel.

❹ **VERSATILITY RULES.** Simply stunning tiebacks—like this brushed-silver concentric circle design—look great on their own, but dress them up with tassels for even more flair. See *page 99* for additional tassel options.

❺ **DRESSED FOR SUCCESS.** These tiebacks in gold, pewter, and iron finishes resemble cufflinks, making them ideal accessories to dress up treatments made with menswear-inspired patterns.

❻ **CARVED AND SWIRLED DETAILS.** This graphic take on the tieback *top* has an architectural quality. The darker finish in the recessed areas makes the design pop. The swirling metal tieback *bottom* has strong graphic appeal; it would look great in a casual or contemporary space.

fabricfundamentals

When choosing window treatments for your home, the style of treatment is only one consideration: The fiber and fabric weave affects how your window treatments will wear, so it is important to understand the differences between various materials. This section features common window treatment fabrics and terminology and is designed to make your shopping experience easier, whether you plan to purchase ready-made window treatments or select fabric for your own creations.

FIBERS Fiber—natural, man-made, or a blend—is raw material knitted or woven to make fabric. Natural fibers include linen, wool, cotton, and silk. These may be used alone or blended with synthetics for added durability. Natural fibers are less likely than synthetics to pill, and they are more luxurious and accept dyes better than man-made materials. Man-made

(synthetic) fibers, such as nylon, rayon, polyester, acrylic, and acetate, tend to wear well and are naturally stain-resistant. Although they are stronger than their natural counterparts, synthetics may pill and are typically not as attractive as natural fibers. Blends of natural and synthetic materials can be less expensive than 100 percent natural fabrics; however, to significantly affect the appearance and performance of a finished product, a natural fiber must make up at least 20 percent of the blend.

FABRIC-BUYING SMARTS
When choosing ready-made window treatments or fabric for do-it-yourself or custom treatments, consider the room where the treatment will hang, who typically uses the room, and how much you're willing to spend.

■ Fabric cost and grade don't necessarily reflect quality. For instance, lower-cost and lower-grade canvas may be more durable than more expensive and higher-grade damask because the canvas is cheaper and less complex to produce. The maker may produce more yards of the canvas than the damask, further lowering the price.

■ Heavy fabrics, such as tapestry, canvas (duck and sailcloth), and woven wool are typically more durable than lightweight fabrics, including satin, taffeta, chintz, and linen.

■ Thread count refers to the number of threads per square inch of fabric (for example, a fabric with a 300 thread count has 300 threads per square inch). Generally, the higher the thread count the more tightly woven the fabric is. The exception is when the threads are especially thick (a heavy wool thread cannot be packed as tightly as a fine cotton thread). When comparing thread counts, consider similar fabrics; the fabric with the higher thread count will wear better and is more likely to resist dirt and stains. Open weaves allow both dirt and liquids to penetrate the fibers, making them more difficult to clean. Tightly woven fabrics help keep liquid spills on the surface, making cleanup easier.

linen

Linen is made from the flax plant. This fiber (and the fabric; see *page 106*) is a popular choice for traditional rooms because of its crisp appearance. Yet in the same way that a linen shirt looks great with blue jeans, a linen window treatment is a good choice for casual settings. Sunlight can weaken this natural fiber, but you can extend its life with linings and interlinings. Linen may be blended with cotton to gain the best attributes from that versatile fiber.

wool

Wool—which comes from the shearing of sheep—has natural elasticity, which makes it a great candidate for upholstery. The fiber's insulating quality makes it a smart choice for windows. Wool fibers have a spiral shape that, when woven, creates air pockets which serve as insulation against winter chills and summer sun.

cotton

Plucked from the cotton plant in popcornlike tufts, cotton can be woven into a wide range of patterns, colors, weights, and textures. This versatile fiber also accepts applications that make it resistant to flame, water, stains, and shrinking.

silk

Silk's reputation for luxury started long ago in China, where threads spun by silkworms were used for fine garments. Like wool, silk has natural elasticity, but it is susceptible to sun damage. Like linen, linings and interlinings will lengthen the life of this often-pricey fiber.

man-made

Nonnatural fibers drape well and are easy to care for. When blended with natural fibers, synthetic fibers boost the strength, longevity, and wrinkle resistance of fabric.

fabric terms to know

Now that you are familiar with the fibers that compose various textiles, it's time to examine the fabrics that work well for window treatments. The following pages are a visual glossary of fabrics, with information on what textiles complement certain decorating styles and which best suit certain uses (such as privacy). Besides fabric types, you will also learn about the most common weaves (dobby, plain weave, satin, twill, and velvet). As you search for ready-made window treatments, visit workrooms, or shop for fabrics to create your own custom treatments, keep this information in mind.

BROCADE. Brocade is a heavy, Jacquard-woven fabric that appears to be embroidered. Woven of silk, cotton, or wool, brocade should be lined to conceal floating yarns on the back.

CHAMBRAY. This tightly woven, lightweight cotton fabric is popular for shirts, and it's equally suitable for window treatments. Chambray works particularly well for flat panels and poufy treatments in casual settings.

CHECKS. Classic checks can be printed or woven into a multitude of fabrics and fibers. Checked fabrics are appropriate for nearly any decorating style, from casual to formal.

CHENILLE. Clipped, twisted yarns give chenille the appearance of caterpillars. This fabric, which can have a matte look or a deep sheen, hangs beautifully as a panel; add a lining for volume.

CHINTZ. Often made of cotton, this fine, plain-weave fabric is glazed to create a surface sheen. Chintz is found in both solids and florals; its weight makes it an excellent choice for treatments with ruffles and poufs.

DAMASK. Floral patterns woven into this satin-weave fabric yield areas of dull and shiny texture. Damask may be woven of cotton, silk, or wool. Mid- to heavyweight damask works well for covered cornices, Roman shades, and panels. Its formal appearance makes it a great candidate for dressy tassels, cords, and trim.

DOBBY. Small raised geometric designs enliven fabrics of the dobby weave, thanks to a special loom attachment. Dobby fabrics are especially good for flat panels because they provide lots of textural interest.

DOTTED SWISS. Tiny dots punctuate this sheer fabric known for its sweet charm. Dotted Swiss fabric is perfect for simple, casual panels in bedrooms and bathrooms; pair it with blinds or opaque panels for privacy.

FRIEZE. This sturdy woven fabric has uncut surface loops, resulting in a warm, heavy drape. The sculptural effect is created by a Jacquard weave.

GROS POINT. Similar to frieze, durable gros point has a minuscule needlepoint look, allowing detail in tiny textural patterns and motifs. This heavy fabric is particularly striking as a covering for a padded cornice.

brocade

chenille

dobby

dotted swiss

chambray

chintz

frieze

checks

damask

gros point

MATELASSÉ. A popular choice for bedding and flat panels, matelassé is a double-woven fabric that features a puckered surface and a spongy feel.

MOIRÉ. The shimmering finish on moiré is created when it is run through rollers that impress a wavy watermark or wood-grain pattern. This fabric looks best in formal settings; use it for flat panels or poufed treatments when you want a solid color with surface interest.

PAISLEY. The curved teardrop paisley pattern was made famous in cashmere shawls brought to Europe from India more than a century ago. Because of its bold, multicolor pattern, use paisley window treatments in a room with solid colors or patterns that share a palette.

PLAID. Stripes and bars of two or more colors cross each other in this classic pattern. Like checks, lively plaids work well in nearly any setting, including country, traditional, and contemporary.

PLAIN WEAVE. Plain weave is the most common weaving method; the lengthwise (warp) and crosswise (weft) threads are equal in weight, so the fabric looks the same on the front and back.

REPP. Repp fabrics are plain-weave fabrics with a ribbed appearance. Whipcord and gabardine are examples of repp fabrics; grosgrain ribbons and taffeta also fit into this category.

SATIN. Satin weaves are created when lengthwise threads float over several crosswise threads. The floating threads—silk, linen, or cotton—reflect light to yield a smooth sheen on the front of the fabric.

IKAT. This Indonesian word means "bundle." To make ikat, bundles of silk or cotton yarn are tied, dyed, and woven into softly blurred geometric patterns. Ikat has a hand-worked look, although modern versions are woven by machine.

JACQUARD. Jacquard fabrics are named for the looms that produce them. These fabrics are recognized for their intricate raised patterns that seem to sit on top of the fabric.

LACE. Bearing flowery motifs or simple geometric patterns, lace is an openwork fabric often made of cotton or a synthetic. This fabric softly diffuses sunlight and is most often used for panels in casual and romantic settings.

LINEN. This strong textural fabric comes from the woody stem of the flax plant. Dye-soaked linen yields pools of lustrous color with a subtle sheen. Linen drapes beautifully and works well as long panels, but the textile wrinkles easily and is typically dry clean only.

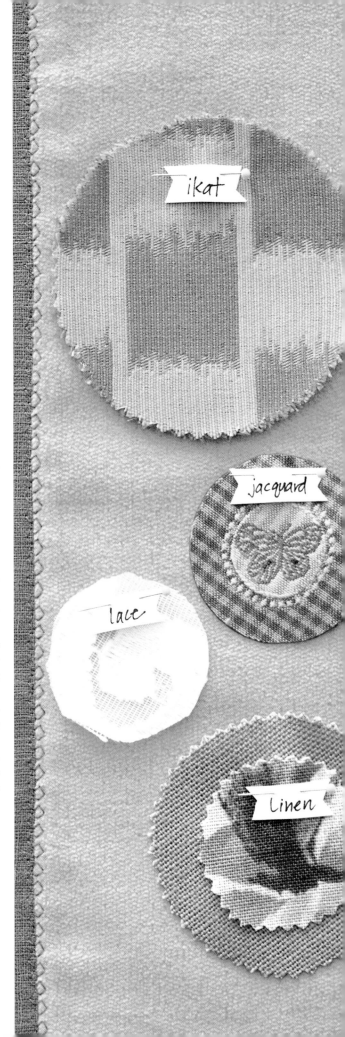

matelassé

plaid

plain weave

repp

moiré

satin

Paisley

terns. Tapestries were once painstakingly made by hand but are now made quickly on a Jacquard loom. Tapestry draperies keep out cold air and glaring sunlight.

TEXTURE. This term can apply to any fabric with an interesting surface, usually created with novelty yarns or weaves (such as repp and dobby fabrics). Here a herringbone pattern is stitched into the fabric for subtle texture. Heavily textured fabrics are best for flat treatments.

TOILE. From France, toiles originally featured pastoral and historical scenes printed in red or navy on ivory-color cotton. Today toiles are printed or woven in a variety of color combinations. This tightly woven fabric works for almost any style of treatment and looks best in traditional, country, or casual chic rooms.

TREE OF LIFE. This fabric is named for its distinct pattern, created with embroidery or crewelwork. Tree of life is best for flat or loosely gathered treatments.

TWILL. Twill is distinguished by progressive, diagonal ridges created when weft threads pass over two or more warp threads. Tightly woven and full bodied, twill works well for windowsill- or floor-length panels; twill doesn't puddle well.

VELVET. Velvet is made either by weaving together two layers of cloth and then cutting them apart, or by weaving fibers over wires and then clipping the resulting loops. Velvet can be woven in silk, cotton, linen, or wool. Velvet works well for formal treatments and blocks drafts and light well.

SHEER. These fluid, see-through fabrics diffuse light well. Sheer panels complement casual and romantic spaces.

SILK. Silk is known for its soft feel and its ability to take dye well. Threads of varying textures are woven to yield the three basic silk fabrics: raw silk, douppioni, and shantung. Silk drapes well and is mildew resistant, but water may stain the fabric. Silk may fade in bright sunlight.

STRIÉ. The term strié refers to fabric with a streaky pattern running the length of the cloth. It's most often seen in plain-weave fabrics patterned with thin stripes, thanks to threads of slightly different colors. Use strié for treatments when you desire subtle visual texture.

TAFFETA. This crisp, luminous fabric rustles when it moves (think wedding dress). Taffeta retains its shape well and is a practical choice for full-bodied draperies.

TAPESTRY. In this heavy, textural fabric, thick threads create pictorial, floral, and geometric pat-

taffeta

toile

tree of life

tapestry

twill

texture

velvet

treatmentsto make

QUICK-SEW PANELS

If you can't find shower curtains that you like, purchase fabric and make your own panels.

Cut panels to the desired size and hem the edges. (Stitch hems or use fusible hem tape, following the directions on *page 117* and on the package.)

To install grommets *left*, you'll need scissors, grommets, a grommet tool, and a hammer. (Or purchase grommets and a grommet punch-pliers.)

Use a fabric marker to mark the locations of the grommets across the top of each curtain panel. Cut holes for the grommets with scissors or use a grommet punch, as directed by the manufacturer. Position half of a grommet ring on each side of the hole; use the grommet tool and the hammer to join the grommet pieces as directed. (Or join them using the grommet pliers.)

STEP BY STEP

1. Cut the ribbon into 12-inch lengths. Thread the ribbon through the grommets on the curtain panels.
2. Prime a wooden rod and brackets; let dry. Paint as desired; let dry. Mount the brackets and hang the rod.
3. Tie the ribbons to the rod as shown *bottom*.

do it yourself

While home centers and department stores abound with options to dress your windows with style, there is nothing more satisfying than doing the work yourself. Regardless of your skill level, you will find projects here perfect for every room of your home.

easy tie-tops Shower curtains already fitted with grommets and tied to a decorative rod with ribbon form this easy no-sew window treatment. The hip Capri-length panels pair with woven blinds to create a relaxed look in this living room.

MATERIALS & TOOLS

*Ribbon, any width and in
    a color that coordinates
    with shower curtains*
2 shower curtains
*Wooden rod, brackets,
    hanging hardware*
Latex primer
*Latex paint, in color that
    coordinates with shower
    curtains*
Measuring tape
Scissors
Paintbrush
Screwdriver

FUN ON A STRING
If door beads aren't your style,
consider these alternatives:
Tie string or cording to a rod,
or wrap one end of long, thin
wires around a rod. Use small
metal clips (or clothespins) to
clip on family photos, postcards,
and other lightweight items at
desired intervals. You could
also hang strips of ribbons
(matching or multiple colors)
in front of the window. Stitch
buttons or other small
adornments to the ribbons.

beaded beauty

Strings of plastic circles transform a plain white sheer curtain
into a fun and funky focal point.

MATERIALS & TOOLS
Sheer curtain panels
Tension rod to mount inside
 window frame
Decorative rod and brackets
Decorative door beads
Screwdriver

STEP BY STEP
1. Thread the sheer curtain
panels onto the tension rod and
install it inside the window
frame.
2. Install the brackets for the
decorative curtain rod and
position the rod on the
brackets.
3. Tie the door beads to the
decorative curtain rod, spacing
them evenly across the rod.

lovelylinens

Napkins and tablecloths transform from dinnertime fare to fair game as fresh-looking window treatments. You won't need a sewing machine to make this low-sew project. Glued-on trim and beads threaded onto wire lend a fun finishing flourish to the valance.

MATERIALS & TOOLS

Tablecloth (sized to suit the window; the tablecloth shown measures 114"×64"), any color and pattern
Coordinating napkins (enough to form a valance and create decorative banding on the panels)
Fusible hem tape
Rod and hanging hardware
Clip-on rings
Decorative trim
Beads
Thin wire
Matching thread
Scissors
Iron and ironing board
Screwdriver
Hot-glue gun and glue sticks
Needle-nose pliers
Hand-sewing needle

STEP BY STEP

1. Cut the tablecloth in half to create two panels. Using the fusible hem tape and following the manufacturer's directions, hem the bottom edge of the panels.

2. Cut the napkins to form the desired width of decorative banding; use fusible hem tape to attach to the outer edges of the panels.

3. Mount the hanging hardware. Clip the rings across the tops of the panels and thread them onto the rod; hang.

4. To create the valance, embellish the remaining napkin edges with trim; use hot glue to secure. Thread the beads onto the thin wire. Use needle-nose pliers to turn the ends of the wire to prevent the beads from slipping off and to create a loop for sewing the wires to the points on the napkins. Hand-stitch the bead-threaded wires onto the points. Drape the napkins over the rod.

TREATMENT ALTERNATIVE

Try this no-sew treatment using tabletop linens: Purchase one or more hemstitch-style table runners (in the desired length and enough runners to cover the width of the window). Thread coordinating ribbons through the cutouts in one short end of each runner and tie it to a decorative rod.

towelcafés

This charming window treatment is made from assorted vintage tea towels, but any kitchen linens will work.

MATERIALS & TOOLS

Tea towels (vintage or new)
Buttons
Café rod and hanging hardware
Matching thread
Measuring tape
Iron and ironing board
Sewing machine or fusible hem tape
Hand-sewing needle
Screwdriver

STEP BY STEP

1. Fold one end of each tea towel to the back to form a rod pocket (the pocket should be about 1½ inches; the bottoms of the finished curtain panels should skim the windowsill when hung). Press and stitch, or secure with fusible hem tape, following the tips *right* and the package directions.
2. Hand-sew buttons 3 inches from the top of each curtain panel.
3. Measure the finished length of the panels; mount the hanging hardware at the appropriate height on either side of the window.
4. Thread the panels onto the rod; hang.

FUSIBLE TAPE AND WEBBING

Here's how to use iron-on fusible webbing or tape to eliminate sewing.

Fusible tape comes in various widths. Narrow tape lets you bond wide ribbon to the fronts of curtain panels, for example. Sheets of fusible webbing allow you to secure appliqués to plain, purchased treatments. You'll also need an iron and an ironing board, scissors, and a cloth measuring tape.

Wash and dry the fabric, then cut the tape or webbing to size and follow the package directions to join the fabric pieces. In most cases, lay the tape or webbing between the fabric layers and press the layers with an iron turned to a low-heat setting; hold the iron in place for the recommended amount of time.

*easy*swag

Red-and-white cotton ticking makes this simple swag a casual complement to the red shutters on this kitchen window.

MATERIALS & TOOLS

1×2 pine mounting board
(see Step 1 for length)
54-inch-wide decorator fabric,
any color and pattern
Measuring tape
Table saw (optional)
Scissors
Fusible hem tape
Iron and ironing board
Staple gun and staples
Screws
Screwdriver

STEP BY STEP

1. To determine the length of the mounting board, measure the width of the window, including the trim; subtract about 6 inches total to accommodate the knots in the valance. Cut the 1×2 pine mounting board to this measurement. *Note: If you do not own a table saw, have the board cut at a home center.*

2. Cut the fabric to a length that is 2½ times the width of the window; cut the fabric in half lengthwise. (Set the other half aside to use for a matching valance on another window or for another project.) Using the fusible hem tape and following the manufacturer's directions, hem the edges of the fabric.

3. Fold the fabric to find the center; staple the top edge of the fabric center to the back edge of the board center. Pull the fabric taut from the center. Staple the top edge of the fabric along the back edge of the board at 1-inch intervals; allow the fabric "tails" to hang freely.

4. To mount the treatment, screw the board to the trim above the window. At each top corner of the window, tie a large, loose knot in the fabric and allow the fabric "tails" to hang down the sides of the window.

PAINTING SHUTTERS

Give worn wooden shutters new life with paint. First prime the shutters with spray primer. Shake the can well and hold it above the surface at the distance recommended by the manufacturer. Point the nozzle toward the shutter, depress the button, and sweep the spray onto the surface, applying a very light layer to prevent drips. Move your arm slowly back and forth to keep the application even. Let the primer dry; flip the shutter over and repeat the process to prime the back side. Paint the shutter with spray paint, using the method described for priming, to cover the shutters with fresh color. Let the shutters dry the recommended amount of time between coats.

sheerdelights

Combining sheers with a colorful band of fabric is an easy way to create a custom look in any room. The 12-inch-deep band on these panels also draws the eye upward to create the illusion of a taller room.

MATERIALS & TOOLS

54-inch-wide sheer fabric (2 yards were used for each 53×72-inch panel; measure window first to determine the finished width and length), any color

54-inch-wide decorator fabric (¾ yard was used for each panel), any color and pattern

Matching thread

Decorative rod and hanging hardware

Measuring tape

Scissors

Iron and ironing board

Sewing machine

Straight pins

Hand-sewing needle

Screwdriver

STEP BY STEP

1. Using the entire fabric width, cut the sheer fabric into 72-inch lengths. Cut the decorator fabric into 24-inch lengths. (Adjust these dimensions as needed to fit your window.)

2. With right sides together and raw edges aligned, press each piece of decorator fabric in half to make 12×54-inch strips; stitch the sides and turn right side out. Press under the raw bottom edges ¼ inch, then an additional ¼ inch.

3. Press under the sides and bottom edge of each 54×72-inch sheer panel ¼ inch, then an additional ¼ inch; hem.

4. Slip 1 inch of each sheer panel inside one decorator fabric band. Pin and topstitch along the bottom of the band to secure the sheer fabric.

5. From the remaining decorator fabric, cut ten 9×1-inch strips for each panel.

With right sides together and raw edges aligned, press the strips in half lengthwise to make 9×½-inch ties. Stitch the long edge and one of the ends; turn right side out and hand-stitch the end closed. Stitch the five pairs of ties evenly along the top edge of each panel.

6. Mount the hanging hardware at the appropriate height on either side of the window. Tie the finished panels onto the curtain rod; hang.

tie-top valance
& shaped roller shade

This fun and colorful window treatment is composed of a flirty valance and an easy-to-make roller shade. You can purchase a roller shade kit at a crafts or fabrics store or through online sources. Most kits contain fusible backing, fusible tape, a bottom slat, a metal telescoping roller that adjusts to fit the width of your window (usually 22 to 36 inches), mounting brackets, screws, and instructions.

VALANCE MATERIALS & TOOLS

54-inch-wide decorator
    fabric, any color and
    pattern
Matching thread
¼-inch-wide coordinating
    ribbon
Decorative rod and
    hanging hardware
Measuring tape
Scissors
Sewing machine
Straight pins
Hand-sewing needle
Screwdriver

VALANCE STEP BY STEP

1. Determine the desired finished width and length of the valance. (Tie-top valances are usually 1½ times the window width.) Cut a piece of decorator fabric 2 inches wider and 4 inches longer than the determined finished measurements.

2. Turn under each side edge ½ inch, then an additional ½ inch; hem. Turn under the bottom edge 1 inch, then an additional 1 inch; hem. Turn under the top edge 1 inch, then an additional 1 inch; hem.

3. Determine the number of ties you would like across the top of the valance; mark each tie position on the valance with a straight pin. Cut the same number of ribbon pieces, cutting each ribbon twice as long as the desired tie length. (The ribbons shown measure about 10 inches long.) Fold each ribbon in half crosswise. Position one ribbon on the back of the valance at each straight pin; position the ribbon fold ½ inch from the valance edge, with the loose ribbon ends toward the top edge. Hand-sew each ribbon to the valance with a small X.

4. Mount the hanging hardware at the appropriate height on either side of the window. Tie the finished valance onto the curtain rod; hang.

ROLLER SHADE MATERIALS & TOOLS

*Fusible fabric roller shade
    kit and mounting
    hardware*
*54-inch-wide decorator
    fabric, any color and
    pattern*
Paper for pattern
Matching thread
*1-inch-wide coordinating
    ribbon*
*¼-inch-wide coordinating
    ribbon*
*Large decorative button,
    any color*
Screwdriver
Measuring tape
Scissors
T-square
Iron and ironing board
Fabric pencil
Sewing machine
Straight pins

ROLLER SHADE STEP BY STEP

1. Mount the shade brackets (included in the roller shade kit) to the wall or inside the window trim. Install the roller mechanism (included in the roller shade kit) in the brackets; adjust for a tight fit.
2. Remove the roller from the brackets and measure the length of the barrel for the shade width. Measure the height from the brackets to the bottom of the window for the shade length. Cut a piece of decorator fabric 1½ inches wider and 18 inches longer than these measurements (center fabric motifs or position patterns appropriately). Cut the fusible backing (included in the roller shade kit) the width of the roller and 12 inches longer than the shade length. The extra length allows for rollover allowance. *Note: Use a T-square to cut the fusible backing and decorator fabric straight and with square corners.*
3. Place the fabric piece right side down on the ironing board; if possible, position a table of the same height next to the board to keep the remaining fabric flat. Position the fusible backing on top of the fabric, centering it across the width of the fabric and aligning the top edges. Following the manufacturer's directions, fuse the backing to the fabric, working from the center to the outside in all directions and overlapping placement of the iron to ensure that the entire area is fused (Diagram 1). Fold over each long side edge ¾ inch toward the fusible backing and fuse to the shade using fusible hem tape (included in the kit).
4. On a piece of paper the same width as the shade, draw the desired edge pattern for the bottom of the shade; cut the pattern. Fold the bottom 6 inches of decorator fabric to the front of the shade, right sides together. Place the paper pattern on the fabric, aligning the bottom edge of the pattern with the fabric fold; mark all cutout shapes of the pattern with a fabric pencil.
5. Machine-stitch along the marked lines. Cut the shaped areas close to the stitches; clip the corners (Diagram 2). Turn right side out along the fold. Press under ½ inch on the raw upper edge of the folded section; sew through all layers close to the folded edge to make a pocket for the slat (Diagram 3).
6. On the front of the shade, pin the 1-inch-wide ribbon along the bottom edges, mitering the corners and turning under each end; topstitch the ribbon to the shade along the edges. Tack a short piece of the ¼-inch-wide ribbon to the back of the shade at the center bottom; secure a button to the end of the ribbon to make a shade pull.
7. Center the unfinished edge of the fabric shade on the roller mechanism and secure following the manufacturer's directions. Install the roller in the brackets.

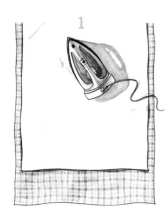

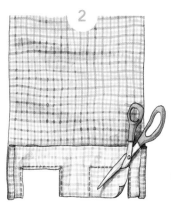

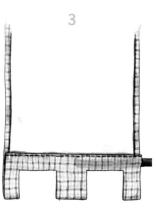

tasseltechniques

silky sensation

A simple, textural silk napkin *above* makes a great tassel decoration when secured over a wooden finial by a string of beads. The skirt is made of fuzzy chenille yarn.

MATERIALS & TOOLS

1 skein (about 98 yards)
*   cotton chenille yarn,*
*   any color*
Heavy perle cotton,
*   coordinating color*
Wooden tassel finial
Two silk cocktail napkins,
*   any color*
Assorted beads, including
*   one string of beads,*
*   any color and material*
Cotton balls or batting
8×8-inch piece of cardboard
Scissors
Monofilament thread
Hand-sewing needle

STEP BY STEP

1. Wrap the skein of cotton chenille yarn around the cardboard. Using an 8-inch-long piece of heavy perle cotton, tie one side of the yarn loops together. On the opposite side of the cardboard, clip the yarn loops to free the ends. Thread both ends of the perle cotton through the needle. Push the needle through the bottom and out the top of the finial.

2. Push the needle through the centers of the two silk cocktail napkins and through a bead. Tie a knot to hold the bead near the finial. Knot the perle cotton again to make a loop several inches long.

3. Make a soft, round head on the wooden finial by stuffing cotton balls or batting between the napkins and the finial. Secure the napkins with perle cotton.

4. Tie the string of beads around the perle cotton-covered finial. Using monofilament thread, randomly affix beads to the chenille skirt.

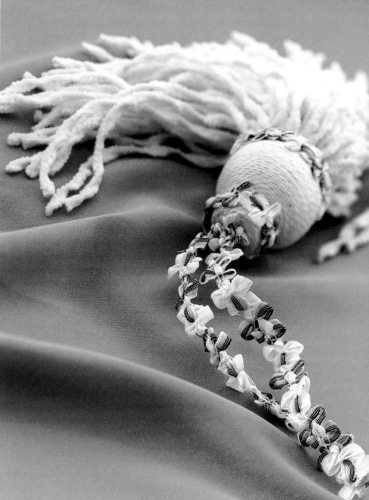

pearlelegance

Pearlized paint coats this three-tier finial *above left*, creating a glamorous partner for the skirt, which is made from strands of pearl trim.

MATERIALS & TOOLS

Three-tier wooden tassel finial
Pearlized-finish acrylic paint, white
White crafts glue
3½ yards prestrung pearls
Sheer ribbon, white, any width
Small paintbrush
5×5-inch piece of cardboard

STEP BY STEP

1. Paint the three-tier wooden finial; let dry.

2. Using the white crafts glue, adhere the pearl "necklaces" to the finial.

3. To make the pearl skirt, wrap 3 yards of pearl strings around the 5×5-inch piece of cardboard. Tie one side of the pearl loops with an 8-inch-long piece of sheer ribbon; do not cut the pearl loops. Slip the pearls off the cardboard. Thread the ribbon ends through the bottom of the finial and out the top; knot the ends near the finial and near the ribbon ends to create the ribbon hanger.

trimmedout

Ready-made trims bring easy-to-add details to any homemade creation. Trim fashioned into flowers of white, black, lime, and yellow creates the color interest on this tassel with a chenille yarn skirt *above right*.

MATERIALS & TOOLS

Wooden tassel finial
White crafts glue
Perle cotton, any color
Satin floral trim, any color
Cotton chenille yarn, any color
Small artist's paintbrush
5×5-inch piece of cardboard
Scissors
Hand-sewing needle

STEP BY STEP

1. Using the artist's paintbrush, apply a thick layer of white crafts glue to the finial. Wrap the perle cotton tightly around the finial, working in small sections to prevent the glue from dripping and drying. Glue the ends inside the finial.

2. Glue bands of the floral trim around the top and bottom of the finial.

3. To make the skirt, wrap the yarn around the 5×5-inch piece of cardboard about 40 times. Using an 8-inch-long piece of floral trim, tie one side of the yarn loops together. On the opposite side of the cardboard, clip the yarn loops to free the ends. Thread both ends of the floral trim through the bottom of the finial and out the top; stitch the ends together to create the hanger.

index

INJUSTICE™2

VOLUME 5

INJUS

TOM TAYLOR
writer

BRUNO REDONDO **DANIEL SAMPERE** **XERMANICO**
pencillers

JUAN ALBARRAN **XERMANICO** **BRUNO REDONDO** **DANIEL SAMPERE**
inkers

REX LOKUS **J. NANJAN**
colorists

WES ABBOTT
letterer

TICE™ 2

VOLUME 5

TYLER KIRKHAM & ARIF PRIANTO
collection cover artists

SUPERMAN created by JERRY SIEGEL and JOE SHUSTER
SUPERGIRL based on the characters created by JERRY SIEGEL and JOE SHUSTER
SUPERBOY created by JERRY SIEGEL
By special arrangement with the Jerry Siegel family

JIM CHADWICK Editor – Original Series
LIZ ERICKSON Assistant Editor – Original Series
JEB WOODARD Group Editor – Collected Editions
ALEX GALER Editor – Collected Edition
STEVE COOK Design Director – Books
MEGEN BELLERSEN Publication Design
ADAM RADO Publication Production

BOB HARRAS Senior VP – Editor-in-Chief, DC Comics
PAT McCALLUM Executive Editor, DC Comics

DAN DiDIO Publisher
JIM LEE Publisher & Chief Creative Officer
BOBBIE CHASE VP – New Publishing Initiatives & Talent Development
DON FALLETTI VP – Manufacturing Operations & Workflow Management
LAWRENCE GANEM VP – Talent Services
ALISON GILL Senior VP – Manufacturing & Operations
HANK KANALZ Senior VP – Publishing Strategy & Support Services
DAN MIRON VP – Publishing Operations
NICK J. NAPOLITANO VP – Manufacturing Administration & Design
NANCY SPEARS VP – Sales
MICHELE R. WELLS VP & Executive Editor, Young Reader

INJUSTICE 2 VOL. 5

Published by DC Comics. Compilation and all new material
Copyright © 2019 DC Comics. All Rights Reserved. Originally
published in single magazine form in INJUSTICE 2 25-30.
Copyright © 2018 DC Comics. All Rights Reserved. All
characters, their distinctive likenesses and related elements
featured in this publication are trademarks of DC Comics. The
stories, characters and incidents featured in this publication
are entirely fictional. DC Comics does not read or accept
unsolicited submissions of ideas, stories or artwork.
DC - a WarnerMedia company.

DC Comics, 2900 West Alameda Ave., Burbank, CA 91505
Printed by LSC Communications, Kendallville, IN, USA.
6/28/19. First Printing.
ISBN: 978-1-4012-9226-3

Library of Congress Cataloging-in-Publication Data is available.

Tom Taylor Writer Daniel Sampere Penciller Juan Albarran Inker Rex Lokus Colorist Wes Abbott Letterer

Cover art by Tyler Kirkham and Arif Prianto

ANYONE WHO CAN STAND, STAND UP.

THE ANDROID COULD COME BACK.

EVERYONE. ON YOUR FEET!

CHECK ON THE FALLEN.

IF THEY CAN STILL FIGHT, GET THEM READY TO FIGHT. IF THEY CAN'T, TELEPORT THEM OUT OF HERE.

AFTERSHOCKS

SUPERBOY?

YOU OKAY, SON?

WHERE'S CASSIE?

CASSIE?

HEY.

YOU OKAY?

YEAH.

LUCKILY, I MANAGED TO CUSHION THE FALL WITH MY HEAD.

YOUR COSTUME IS AMAZING.

THANK YOU.

SERIOUSLY, I LOVE IT! IT'S LIKE YOU'RE COMPENSATING FOR SO MUCH AND YOU'RE TRYING TO MAKE YOURSELF FEEL BETTER.

HEY.

NAAAW. YOU EVEN GAVE YOURSELF A BIG STAR IN THE MIDDLE! GOOD FOR YOU.

BOOSTER. ARE YOU IN CONTACT WITH BLUE BEETLE? WHERE IS HE?

BATS...

THERE YOU GO.

THANK YOU.

UM... THANK YOU.

WHO *ARE* YOU?

I'M NOT SUPPOSED TO SAY. BUT I'M HERE TO HELP.

IS THAT ENOUGH?

I SUPPOSE IT WILL HAVE TO BE.

I'M JAIME.

YOU'RE...AH... STILL HOLDING ITS BRAIN.

YES, IT... REMINDS ME OF SOMETHING. SOMETHING EVIL.

IF IT WERE TO FALL INTO THE WRONG HANDS...

WELL, IT'S IN *YOUR* HAND NOW. WHAT ARE YOU GOING TO DO WITH IT?

GSSH

IT'S DONE!

AMAZO'S OFFLINE.

NO!

THP

SMMK SMMK

HNG!

SHLK

JASON!

RRRR!

YOU KILLED IVO.

GRANDFATHER. HE WAS SABOTAGING--

IT DOESN'T MATTER!

WE NEEDED HIS MIND TO SAVE THE WORLD, AND YOU PUT A BULLET THROUGH IT.

I'M SORRY. I...

I CAN'T SAVE YOU THIS TIME, CHILD.

WHAT?

GRANDFATHER?

GRANDFATHER!

I STOOD AGAINST GRODD FOR YOU, AL GHUL.

I KNOW, SOLOVAR.

I DIVIDED MY KINGDOM FOR YOU.

FOR THE BETTER WORLD YOU PROMISED FOR MY PEOPLE.

FOR MY FAMILY.

AND *YOUR* FAMILY TOOK THAT AWAY.

IT'S OKAY. THE ROBOT'S DEALT WITH.

WHAT DO YOU MEAN IT'S DEALT WITH? DID YOU TAKE IT OUT?

AH... NO. I THINK IT MALFUNCTIONED.

MALFUNCTIONED?

YEAH. WE WERE ON THE MOON, AND BOOM!

WELL, NOT BOOM. THERE'S NO SOUND UP THERE. BUT... YOU KNOW, IT BLEW UP.

ADAM. YOU CAN FLY?

YES.

GOOD. WE'RE LEAVING.

WAIT.

"Two Meetings, One Bullet"

Tom Taylor Writer **Bruno Redondo** Penciller **Juan Albarran** Inker **Rex Lokus** Colorist **Wes Abbott** Letterer

Cover art by **Bruno Redondo** and **Alejandro Sanchez**

I'M UNABLE TO ACCESS MY MONITORS AND 37 CAMERAS IN THE EAST WING OF WAYNE MANOR.

SORRY. I HAVE TO TAKE THIS.

IS EVERYTHING OKAY, BRUCE?

MY SECURITY SYSTEM AT WAYNE MANOR HAS BEEN AFFECTED. IT HAS SEVERAL FAIL-SAFES. THIS SHOULDN'T HAPPEN.

UM... HAVE YOU TRIED TURNING IT ON AND OFF AGAIN?

IT'S A LITTLE MORE COMPLICATED THAN THAT.

HAVE YOU TRIED TURNING IT ON AND OFF AGAIN?

I'VE DONE A FULL RESET OF WAYNE MANOR. THE CAMERAS HAVEN'T COME BACK ONLINE. NO OTHER SYSTEMS ARE AFFECTED.

SELINA? ALFRED?

THEY'RE IN THE WING THAT WENT DARK.

EXTERNAL MONITORING? SATELLITE?

I'VE UTILIZED BOTH. NO SIGN OF TRESPASSERS OR DAMAGE.

HAVE YOU TRIED TELECOMMUNICATIONS, BROTHER EYE?

I'VE REPEATEDLY CALLED SELINA KYLE'S CELL PHONE AND THE LANDLINE AT WAYNE MANOR.

THERE'S NO ANSWER.

"...I'LL BE BACK SOON."

OTHER EYE.

LAST KNOWN LOCATIONS OF SELINA AND ALFRED?

ALFRED PENNYWORTH WAS IN HIS MASTER BEDROOM.

SELINA KYLE WAS EN ROUTE...

NO...
NO!

TWO MEETINGS, ONE BULLET

"Hate"
Tom Taylor Writer **Xermanico** Artist **J. Nanjan** Colorist **Wes Abbott** Letterer

Cover art by **Tyler Kirkham** and **Arif Prianto**

"TWO HUNDRED GREEN LANTERNS.

"CHOSEN AS THE FINEST, MOST FEARLESS WARRIORS IN THE UNIVERSE.

"ALL GONE.

IN PART, BECAUSE OF YOU.

HOW DO YOU PLEAD...?

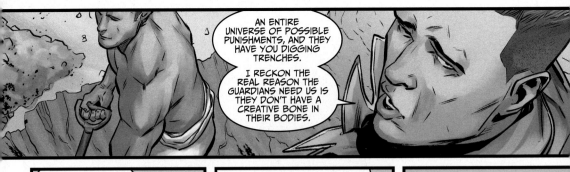

AN ENTIRE UNIVERSE OF POSSIBLE PUNISHMENTS, AND THEY HAVE YOU DIGGING TRENCHES.

I RECKON THE REAL REASON THE GUARDIANS NEED US IS THEY DON'T HAVE A CREATIVE BONE IN THEIR BODIES.

CAN YOU IMAGINE THEM ON THEIR OWN? "WE WILL FIGHT THE FORCES OF DARKNESS."

"WHAT WITH, MY GIANT-HEADED, REPRESSED COMPANION? WHAT SHALL WE CRAFT FROM THE LIGHT?"

"AH. WHAT ABOUT A PERFECTLY GEOMETRIC CUBE?"

"CURSES. DARKSEID HAS MOVED AROUND THE CUBE. WHAT SHOULD WE DO NOW?"

"UM... QUICKLY! ANOTHER CUBE!"

"TOO LATE. DARKSEID IS SOMEHOW PULLING MY GARGANTUAN BRAIN OUT OF MY TINY NOSTRIL!"

"AGHHH! MY RIGID, UNIMAGINATIVE BRAIN!!!"

HEH

"...I SPENT A WEEK ON MOGO.

"I BREATHED HIS AIR...

"...SWAM IN HIS OCEANS...

"...RAN AND FLEW ALONGSIDE ALL THE ANIMALS THAT LIVED UPON HIM.

"THEY ALL BURNED WITH MOGO."

MY MOTHER
OOK HER OWN LIFE.
DIDN'T SHE?

DO NOT--

SO SHE
WOULDN'T HAVE
TO SPEND IT
WITH YOU.

SORANIK.

SORANIK!

WHAT
IS IT?

WE HAVE A
GREEN LANTERN
DOWN.

WHAT?

WE DON'T
KNOW WHAT DID
IT BUT--

CRMCH

WELL, THIS JUST GOT A WHOLE LOT MORE ENTERTAINING.

HEY.

SORANIK. I KNOW HOW EASY HE IS TO HATE, BUT YOU HAVE TO CALM DOWN.

YOU'RE TOO GOOD A LANTERN TO GO DOWN THIS PATH.

OH, GET OUT OF THE WAY.

I'M NOT GOING TO KILL HIM.

I'M NOT YOU, JORDAN. I'M NOT A MURDERER.

AND I AM DEFINITELY NOT MY FATHER.

YOU'RE SO DISAPPROVING, DAUGHTER, YET LOOK AT YOU. BEATING A PRISONER IN YOUR CARE. WE'RE CLEARLY NOT SO DIFFERENT.

SORANIK. ARE YOU THERE...?

TOMAR-RE IS DEAD.

WHAT?

HE WAS INVESTIGATING A LIFE SIGN ON THE DARK SIDE OF THE PLANET.

HE'S BEEN ATTACKED.

BY WHAT?

WHATEVER IT IS, IF IT TOOK DOWN TOMAR-RE BEFORE HE COULD EVEN RAISE AN ALARM, IT'S A THREAT TO EVERYONE HERE.

YOU SHOULD CALL TO OA. EVACUATE THIS PRISON.

DO YOU TAKE ORDERS FROM YOUR PRISONER NOW, WARDEN?

THIS IS NOT THE TIME FOR PRIDE TO TRUMP SENSE. WE NEED TO GO BEFORE--

MULTIPLE BEINGS ARE APPROACHING THE PLANET.

LANTERNS. FALL BACK TO THE PRISON COMPLEX! FALL BACK TO--

"Rage on Harring"

Tom Taylor Writer **Daniel Sampere** Penciller **Juan Albarran** and **Daniel Sampere** Inkers
Rex Lokus Colorist **Wes Abbott** Letterer

Cover art by **Daniel Sampere** and **Alejandro Sanchez**

KILL THEM, ATROCITUSSSS?

RAGE ON HARRING

HAL.

THAT'S CLEARLY A TALKING EVIL KITTY.

YES.

LIKE, NOT SOME KIND OF ALIEN FELINE CREATURE, JUST A MALEVOLENT, TALKY HOUSE CAT IN A LITTLE SUIT.

YES.

THAT'S ONE OF THE WEIRDEST THINGS I'VE EVER SEEN.

AND I'M SAYING THAT AS A SPECTRAL MANIFESTATION OF YOUR OWN GUILT.

GREEN LANTERNSSSS!

KILL THEM!

NO!

YEAH. THAT WOULDN'T BE A GOOD THING.

LET GO OF ME, JORDAN!

DON'T!

LET IT GO!

HAL JORDAN OF EARTH.

YOU HAVE GREAT RAGE IN YOUR HEART.

THD

JORDAN?

I...CAN'T... CONTROL THIS.

TAKE SINESTRO... GET TO OA.

YOU BELONG TO THE RED LANTERN CORPS.

RUN!

OA. HOME TO THE GUARDIANS OF THE UNIVERSE AND THE GREEN LANTERN CORPS.

SORANIK!

WHAT HAPPENED ON HARRING?

RED LANTERNS DESTROYED THE PRISON. IT'S GONE.

WE BARELY MANAGED TO ESCAPE.

HOW *DID* YOU MANAGE TO ESCAPE?

HAL SAVED US.

JORDAN? HOW?

HE TOOK A RED RING. HE WAS ABLE TO CONTROL HIS RAGE LONG ENOUGH TO DEFEND US.

WHERE IS HE NOW?

"WHERE IS HAL JORDAN?"

HRAARGH!!

RELEASE ME!

ATROCITUS. WE SHOULD KILL HIM! HE USED OUR OWN POWER AGAINST US.

HE USED IT WELL. HE USED IT WITH MORE FURY AND CONTROL THAN MOST OF YOU. HE--

SHLK

RAARGH!

EAT YOU!

WAIT!

...IS NOT THE FIRST [TIME] YOU'VE WIELDED A RING, IS IT?

I KNOW WHO YOU ARE.

YOU'RE HAL JORDAN.

YOUR BETRAYAL OF THE GUARDIANS, THE DEAD GREEN LANTERNS LEFT IN YOUR WAKE...

NEWS OF YOUR TREACHERY AND VIOLENCE HAS SPREAD ACROSS THE UNIVERSE.

OH. YAY.

CONGRATS, JORDAN. YOU'RE A BIG NAME IN INTERGALACTIC PSYCHOPATH CIRCLES.

DO WE HAVE TO TEAR YOU TO PIECES, OR WILL YOU JOIN YOUR RAGE WITH OURS, HAL JORDAN?

JUST TELL THEM WHAT THEY WANT TO HEAR, HAL.

DON'T BE, YOU KNOW, *YOU.*

I WILL!

FINE! HE IS ONE OF US. NOW WE SHOULD BE CHASING SINESTRO AND THE GREEN LANTERNS WHO TOOK HIM.

NO.

YOU MAY BE THE ONLY CREATURE ALIVE WHO HATES SINESTRO MORE THAN I, BLEEZ. BUT WE NEED TO THINK BIGGER.

IF THEY REACH THE SAFETY OF OA...?

THEY *WILL* REACH OA. THEY MAY BE THERE ALREADY. BUT THEY WILL NOT FIND SAFETY THERE.

WHAT ARE YOU SUGGESTING, ATROCITUS? EVEN OU[R] COMBINED RAGE CAN'[T] STAND AGAINST THE GUARDIANS.

I HAVE MADE CONTACT WITH SOMETHING. I KNOW WHAT CAN TEAR THEM DOWN.

MY FAMILY, MY WORLD, WAS ENDED BY THE GUARDIANS' MANHUNTERS. IT IS TIME THEY PAID THE PRICE.

IT IS TIME FOR OA TO FALL...

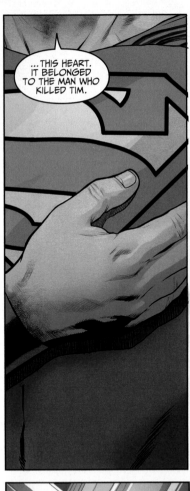

...THIS HEART. IT BELONGED TO THE MAN WHO KILLED TIM.

AH.

AND, YOU THINK EVIL CAN BE TRANSPLANTED VIA ORGANS?

I DON'T KNOW...

WELL, WHICH ORGANS? ALL OF THEM?

CAN EVIL BE TRANSPLANTED VIA A KIDNEY?

HOW MUCH EVIL IS CONTAINED IN THE AVERAGE SPLEEN?

YOU'RE RIGHT. IT'S STUPID.

IT'S NOT STUPID.

STARRO THE CONQUEROR IS A RED LANTERN...

RIGHT, WELL, THIS IS PRETTY MUCH THE SINGLE WORST THING IMAGINABLE.

OOK. I DON'T
ALLY KNOW THE
OMMUNITY THAT
L. I'M NOT SURE
HO I COULD
SUGGEST.

JAIME.

I MEAN,
STEEL
SEEMS
COOL.

JAIME...

AND I WOULD
HAVE SUGGESTED
AQUALAD RIGHT
UP TO THE POINT
WHEN HE MURDERED
THE ENTIRE
GOVERNMENT--

JAIME!

WHAT?!

WE'D LIKE
YOU TO TRY
OUT FOR THE
TITANS.

SOMETHING'S COMING!

YOU MANAGED TO EMBARRASS A ROBOT.

THAT'S IMPRESSIVE... SKEETS?

WHAT? WHERE?!

GET YOUR DEFENSES UP!

GET--

K O R

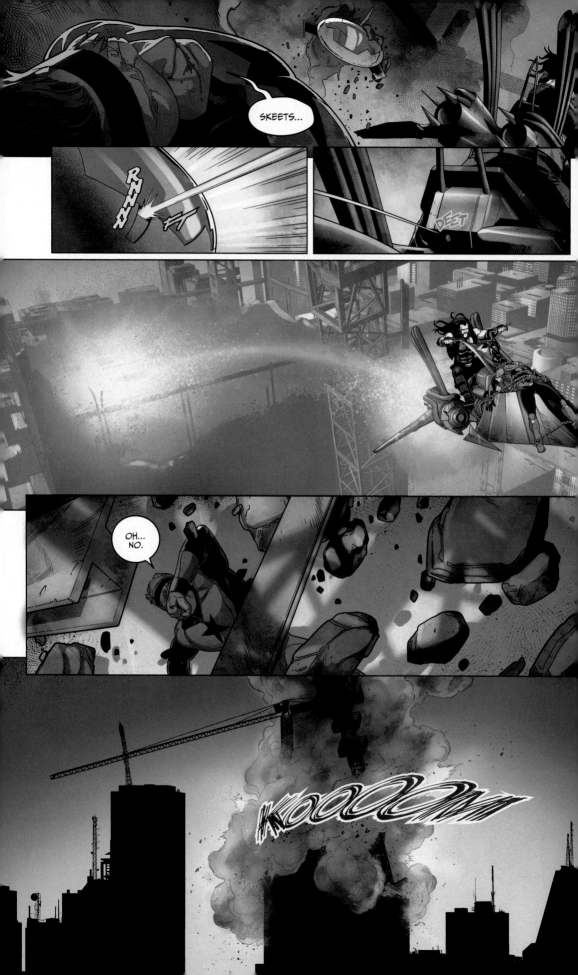

ARE YOU SURE YOU CAN DO THIS?

KID. I'M A THIEF FROM THE FUTURE. THAT WOULD BE LIKE ME ASKING IF YOU CAN STEAL A HORSE.

SKEETS? DO YOU KNOW HOW TO START THIS THING?

Tom Taylor Writer Xermánico Artist J. Nanjan Colorist Wes Abbott Letterer

Cover art by **Tyler Kirkham** and **Arif Prianto**

TYLER KIRKHAM
arf

"YOU ARE THE ONLY BEING WHO CAN STAND AGAINST STARRO.

"THE CONQUEROR, CONSUMED WITH RAGE.

ATTACK ON OA

"HIS SPORES FUSED WITH HATE."

HAL.

"EVERY CREATURE HIS STARS TOUCH WILL BE INFECTED.

"STARRO'S ANGER WILL BECOME THEIRS. THEY WILL TEAR THEMSELVES APART."

HAL.

I KNOW YOUR MIND IS CLOUDED, BUT THEY'RE GOING TO DESTROY OA. YOU KNOW THIS.

AND STARRO WON'T STOP THERE. HE'LL WIPE OUT THE UNIVERSE, MAN.

EARTH.

CAROL.

"...BUT HE CANNOT ESCAPE STARRO."

FASTER, HAL!

HNNG!

SHLK

DON'T LET IT TAKE HOLD, JORDAN!

SINESTRO PLAYED YOU LIKE AN IDIOT. SUPERMAN MADE YOU HIS PUPPET.

ARE YOU GOING TO LET ANOTHER THING CONTROL YOU?

THD

YES! THAT'S IT! KEEP HITTING YOURSELF.

THD

KEEP HITTING YOURSELF!

FWOOM

WHOOM

YES!

HAL, FOR THE RECORD, I KNOW I'M NOT REAL, BUT WATCHING YOU PUNCH YOURSELF REPEATEDLY IN THE FACE WAS INCREDIBLE.

IF A MANIFESTATION OF YOUR OWN SHAME COULD LOOK SATISFIED, THIS IS WHAT IT WOULD LOOK LIKE.

SORANIK!

WHAT IS IT?

SCOUTS ARE REPORTING SOMETHING APPROACHING OA AT HIGH SPEED.

THE GUARDIANS HAVE REQUESTED A DEFENSIVE PERIMETER AROUND THE PLANET.

SAYD?

IT'S ALL RIGHT. STAND DOWN. I WILL DEAL WITH HIM.

WHO?

"HAL JORDAN."

THAT IS FAR ENOUGH.

NO! YOU HAVE TO LISTEN. YOU HAVE TO--

YOUR MIND IS CLOUDED BY THE RING YOU WEAR.

WE WILL WORK TO REMOVE ITS INFLUENCE AS WE--

RAARGH

SHUT UP AND LISTEN, YOU ARROGANT @#$%!

I'M NOT SURE INSULTS AND ATTACKS ARE REALLY THE BEST WAY TO GET YOUR MESSAGE ACROSS, MAN.

SERIOUSLY. YOU GONNA KILL THEM ALL AND HOPE THEY LISTEN AFTER THAT?

GONNA HAVE TO TRY SOMETHING MORE DRASTIC TO GET THROUGH TO THEM, HAL.

HAL JORDAN. IF YOU ATTEMPT LETHAL FORCE, WE WILL BE FORCED TO--

NAArGHHH!

IT'S ALWAYS AMPUTATION WITH YOU...

LISTEN TO ME! BEFORE IT'S TOO LATE.

THE RED LANTERNS. THEY'VE TAKEN--

THEY'VE TAKEN STARRO THE CONQUEROR.

CHOOM

CHOOM

HEY, BASTICHES.

BWWWOOOP BWOOOP

GUYS...WE'VE CRASHED INTO THE TESTOSTERONE-FUELED PERSONIFICATION OF THE 1980s.

BWOOP BWOOOP

OPEN THE BAY DOORS.

LAST GUY WHO WENT UP AGAINST ME WEARIN' THAT SYMBOL CAUSED ME A BIT A TROUBLE.

...DECIDED I WASN'T GONNA GET IN TROUBLE AGAIN.

BRANG

THERE IS NO NEED FOR THIS.

THESE BEINGS ARE NOT OUR ENEMY, LOBO.

SKEETS? WHAT ARE WE DEALING WITH?

BWWOOOP BWOOOP

HIS NAME IS METRON. HE IS A NEW GOD. HE HOLDS UNPARALLELED KNOWLEDGE AND A GREAT UNDERSTANDING OF ENGINEERING AND MECHANICS. HE IS ONE OF THE MOST INTELLIGENT BEINGS IN THE UNIVERSE.

BWWOOOP BWOOOP

REALLY? CAN HE HEAR ME OUT THERE?

HE SHOULDN'T BE ABLE TO. BUT HE'S PROBABLY CREATED A POCKET FOR SOUND TO TRAVEL OR SOME SUCH. REASON HAS A HABIT OF BENDING AROUND GODS. AS A ROBOT BUILT ON LOGIC, I CAN'T TELL YOU HOW FRUSTRATING--

GREAT METRON.

YES.

I UNDERSTAND YOU ARE ONE OF THE GREATEST MINDS IN EXISTENCE.

YES.

BWOOP BWOOOP

COULD YOU... AH, COULD YOU TURN THE ALARM OFF IN THIS THING?

BWWWOOOP BWWOO-- BEEP BEEP

OH MY GOD. THANK YOU.

I CAN'T BELIEVE YOU GUYS CAME OUT HERE FOR ME.

JAIME? WHAT'S HAPPENING HERE?

I APPARENTLY HAVE TO SAVE THE UNIVERSE.

WHAT?

STARRO THE CONQUEROR, ALREADY FORMIDABLE, HAS BEEN CORRUPTED BY ANGER.

NOW A WAR HAS BEGUN. A WAR WHICH WILL SPELL THE END OF THE UNIVERSE IF IT IS LOST.

THE SCARAB AND ITS BEARER HAVE DEFEATED STARRO BEFORE, THOUSANDS OF YEARS AGO...

...IT FALLS TO THE BLUE BEETLE TO CONQUER THE CONQUEROR AGAIN.

AND WILL YOU BE FIGHTING IN THIS WAR WITH US?

I WILL NOT INTERCEDE DIRECTLY.

BUT THE MOBIUS CHAIR CAN TRAVEL ACROSS SPACE INSTANTLY. I WILL TRANSPORT THE BLUE BEETLE TO WAR.

AND WE WILL FIGHT BY HIS SIDE.

UM...CAN WE GET A LIFT?

YES.

WHERE ARE WE GOING...?

WE HAVE ARRIVED. STARRO AWAITS.

YOU GET ONE A THEM STARS ON YOU, IT'S OVER. YOU'RE HIS.

OKAY. TITANS?

WE ARE READY.

YEAH. IF A GIANT STARFISH HAS BOLLOCKS, THE MAIN MAN WILL FIND 'EM AN' TEAR 'EM OFF.

LET'S GO.

JAIME?

HE'S IN HERE.

JAIME?

I CAN'T
DO THIS.

YES.
YOU
CAN.

BATMAN
THINKS...

OH GOD!
THAT GUY.

YOU KNOW WHAT?
BATS CLAIMS HE HAS
NO POWERS, BUT THAT'S
@#$%. HIS SUPERPOWER
IS FILLING HIS FELLOW
HEROES WITH CRIPPLING
INSECURITIES.

SERIOUSLY,
EVERY SINGLE
ROBIN GETS A
PAIR OF TIGHTS AND
AN INFERIORITY
COMPLEX.

KID. LOOK AT ME.
WE'RE GONNA WIN.

HOW DO YOU
KNOW?

BECAUSE,
IF WE DON'T, TED
KORD DIED FOR
NO REASON.

WHAT ARE YOU TALKING ABOUT?

I TOLD YOU, I TRIED TO COME BACK FROM THE FUTURE. I TRIED TO SAVE HIM.

BUT THEY WOULDN'T LET ME. TEDDY HAD TO DIE. THAT'S WHAT THEY TOLD ME.

NOW I KNOW WHY...

FOR YOU.

OH, DON'T LOOK AT ME LIKE THAT.

I'M NOT SAYING IT WAS YOUR FAULT. BUT I GUESS IT SOUNDED LIKE THAT.

SORRY. I CHOSE MY WORDS FOR DRAMATIC IMPACT, RATHER THAN ACCURACY.

IT'S NOT YOUR FAULT, JAIME. IT'S THE UNIVERSE'S FAULT.

FOR SOME REASON, IF TED HAD LIVED, YOU WOULDN'T BE IN A PLACE TO SAVE EVERYTHING.

SO, HERE'S THE THING. YOU'RE GOING TO GO OUT THERE. AND I'LL BE RIGHT BESIDE YOU.

YOU AND THAT THING ON YOUR BACK ARE SOMEHOW GOING TO STAND UP TO A WORLD CONQUEROR AND SAVE THE UNIVERSE.

SKEETS?

YES?

THAT MESSAGE TED LEFT FOR ME--COULD YOU PLAY THE RELEVANT BIT?

CERTAINLY.

...THERE'S THIS KID. JAIME. HE'S SPECIAL.

YOU CAN SEE IT. HE'S ACTUALLY GONNA BE THE KIND OF HERO WE ALWAYS PRETENDED WE'D BE ONE DAY.

YOU READY?

NO.

YOU GOING OUT THERE ANYWAY?

YEP.

OKAY.

SKEETS, OPEN THE BAY DOORS.

BOOSTER?

YEAH?

WHAT TED SAID ABOUT PRETENDING TO BE A HERO... THAT WAS ABSOLUTE @#$%%$#.

HE WAS A HERO.

OH, I KNOW.

HE WAS MINE.

LOBO — INJ2

BRUNO REDONDO
18

METRON character design by Xermanico

METRON

METRON'S CHAIR.

ATROCITUS

STARFIRE - INJ2

BRUNO
REDONDO
18

WONDER GIRL - INJ 2